King of Burglars

The Heist Stories of Max Shinburn

By Maximilian Schoenbein

[aka Max Shinburn, Mark Shinborn]

Edited with a foreword by Jerry Kuntz

Wickham House

Warwick, New York

MAXIMILIAN SCHOENBEIN

Maximilian Schoenbein (Max Shinburn)

National Portrait Gallery, Smithsonian Institution; gift of Pinkerton's, Inc.

CONTENTS

Foreword

The following stories first appeared in Sunday editions of the *Boston Herald* newspaper between April and June, 1913. They were written by Maximilian Schoenbein, then in his 70s, three years prior to his death in 1916. Schoenbein was better known to the public as Max Shinburn, although these articles appeared under a less-frequently employed alias, Mark Shinborn. Schoenbein was the most infamous bank robber of the 1860s, responsible for thefts that totaled in the millions. He was renowned not only for his skill as a sneak thief and safe-blower, but also for his haughty, elitist attitude. His affectations later led him to purchase a title of nobility in Europe—he was briefly "Baron Schindle of Monaco"--but subsequent financial and legal missteps reduced him to the humble circumstances that resulted in the need to write these articles. Schoenbein ended his days in the confines of a Boston charity home for former convicts.

The articles appeared just weeks after the syndicated newspaper articles written about the same generation of criminals by Sophie Lyons, one of the most notorious pickpockets and molls of late nineteenth-century America. Sophie's articles were later collected and edited in book version under the title *The Amazing Adventures of Sophie Lyons, Queen of the Burglars; or, Why Crime Does Not Pay,* reflecting her efforts not only to reform her life but the lives of other former convicts, and to alleviate the misfortunes of their families. Many critics thought Lyons' writings glamorized crooks, and only added a moral message as an aside. Those same skeptics would likely have been aghast at Schoenbein's articles, which expressed no apologies for a life of crime and no remorse over those he victimized. One must wonder how his articles ever saw print in a Boston newspaper, as that city was regarded as a bastion of public morality. Even today, a reader can sense how deeply subversive Schoenbein's collected writings were.

This may partially explain why these articles were never syndicated, nor collected and published in book form. For over a century they have been "lost" in the sense they that were never reprinted separately; and never referenced in bibliographies. Since the advent of digitized newspaper databases, these articles may have even eluded some 21st-century researchers, since they were published under the rare alias "Mark Shinborn." Each of the eleven articles contains at least one true-crime "heist" story, and rank among the earliest examples of that genre, now a staple of popular culture. Each article contains at least one tale of the planning, execution, complication, and escape from a robbery; and several contain elements of the ridiculous. Also to be found are several tales of clever prison escapes, another standard crime-story genre.

"Mark Shinborn Tells Story of His Greatest Peril" is a classic heist story, presenting the unforgettable image of a crawling escape across a half-built bridge high above a river gorge—at night, in a blizzard, carrying packs of loot. It deserves a place among the great adventure stories in American popular culture. The other stories suffer in comparison, although "A Wad of Bills Gets Mark Shinborn Out of a Tight Place" may be one of the most subversive tales ever set in the United States: every single figure in the story is corrupt, starting with the alleged victim of a hold-up for which Schoenbein was mistakenly arrested.

Corruption is a major theme running through the articles. In several places, Schoenbein refers to a "10 per cent protection" paid to New York City detectives on robberies committed outside the city, in return for ignoring or diverting requests for assistance from those victimized jurisdictions. Through these pay-offs, crooks could congregate in New York City without fear of arrest. However, if violence had been involved in the robbery, the New York cops would consider it "blood money," and all deals were off. Another unwritten rule was that bank robbers would not target institutions within the city—a code that a few ignored, though Schoenbein was careful in that respect. In "How Four Gangs Sought to Rob the Wolfeboro, N.H., Bank," Schoenbein devotes the opening columns to detail the mechanics of New York City graft in the 1860s.

Schoenbein himself was far from admirable, a point he lets slip at several junctions in these stories. In "How Shinborn Cleaned Up $20,000 At Springfield," he expresses no qualms at all about stealing a safe full of payday envelopes intended for railroad workers. That same story concludes with Schoenbein threatening his friend and partner for a share of a robbery in which he did not participate. In several instances he berates other crooks for their mistakes but admits few of his own. He accepts or declines participation in various robberies with imperious declarations. He eschewed the use of violence, but not based on any moral qualms--he merely believed that heavy-handed techniques increased the risk of capture and added extra years to sentencing penalties.

Schoenbein's elitism, combined with rumors of his treachery towards fellow criminal mastermind Adam Worth, likely tarnished his reputation as a preeminent criminal. His relationship with Worth was complex. Schoenbein devotes his first two stories to the exploits of Worth, whom he describes as an old friend. Worth, who died in 1902, likely would have rolled over in his grave to hear Schoenbein claim him as a friend and equal, for it was Schoenbein--acting as an informer against Worth--that kept Worth in a Belgian prison for years and broke his health. Schoenbein's detailed information concerning Worth's past crimes was offered to reduce his own time in jail. Such backstabbing was not uncommon among the thieves of that era, but the enmity between Worth and Schoenbein is especially notable since both men were once at the pinnacle of their profession.

Similarly, George Miles White appears in many of Schoenbein's tales as an expert, independent thief. White found religion in later life and reformed, writing two books about his experiences. In his autobiographical writings, White places some blame on his descent into a life of crime on Max Schoenbein, inasmuch that Schoenbein presented himself as a Deputy Marshal and hired White as a rig driver to take him to scout possible robbery targets. Schoenbein's account matches White's, in that both placed more blame on a third man, James Cummings, for White's subsequent misfortunes. Like Adam Worth, George White died several years before Schoenbein published his stories, and would not have appreciated the dredging up of his past sins.

Schoenbein was notably reticent about revealing too much of his personal life in these stories. There are a few references to lovers and a wife, but other than that we have no sense of any strong attachments. He never mentions his German parents, his upbringing and education, or any siblings. In "A Wad of Bills Gets Mark Shinborn Out of a Tight Place," Schoenbein mentions coming to the United States from Canada in the late 1850s; this is earlier than the 1860/1861 date given by other sources. His early years in the United States were spent as a house and store thief, activities that supported his lifestyle as a gambler. He was naturalized as an American citizen in 1869, while at the height of his bank-robbing career, though it is doubtful that he was inspired by patriotism.

Schoenbein's stories offer a detailed look at the mechanics of early bank robberies and safe-breaking techniques. Although not mentioned in these pages, Schoenbein is credited with the invention of a thin foil or paper device that was placed underneath the dial of combination locks; during opening of the locks by the legitimate safe owners, light imprints of the tumbler number positions would be recorded. The thief would then recover the device and learn the combination. In the late 1870s, this device was adopted by George L. Leslie, the man who briefly inherited Schoenbein's mantle as the king of bank robbers.

Still, it is not the techniques of the thief that make the strongest impression in these stories. Instead, the reader sees evidence of a widespread, perfidious criminal underworld in American society, populated by professional thieves and counterfeiters preying upon financial institutions, corporations, and ordinary citizens. This subculture operated unabated during the Civil War. In Schoenbein's phrase, its members had "no interest in the fate of the country." Some used army enlistment bounties to enrich themselves.

Gambling—not baseball—was the national pastime. Under the right circumstances, police detectives could be neutralized with graft payments. Ordinary citizens abetted criminals by providing them information, passing counterfeit bills, and selling their stolen goods. Yet somehow, Schoenbein makes this unsettling view of society entertaining by focusing on the momentary thrill and risk of each theft and escape. The reader has little choice but to root for the success of the "King of Burglars," a title bestowed on him by newspapers as well as America's foremost detectives.

--Jerry Kuntz *August 2018*

1 THE REAL STORY OF THE STOLEN GAINSBOROUGH PORTRAIT

I cannot recall any crime in the whole list of the last half-century that created greater excitement or held the interest of the public on both sides of the Atlantic for a longer period than the theft of the Gainsborough portrait, now generally known as the Stolen Duchess.

That was the work of my old associate, Adam Worth, a native of Massachusetts, promoter of robberies that ran into the millions and prime mover in the remarkable Kimberley diamond affair, the looting of the Boylston Bank in Boston and other shady transactions too numerous to mention.

Personally I had no hand in the stealing of the picture, but I saw it later in Worth's possession, helped to hide it in London, and heard the story of how it was secured from Worth's own lips. The tale he told me differs in many respects from the account which usually has been accepted as the true one.

There is no doubt that Adam was one of the brainiest and most unscrupulous crooks of his time, or, for that matter, of any other time. He made very few failures owing to the fact that he was endowed with a rare combination of imagination and executive ability. He could plan and carry out his plans with equal skill. He knew, too, how to wait for the appropriate moment, and it was this peculiar quality of patience that enabled him to make the picture pay him for his trouble even after a lapse of 25 years.

I suppose it was the mystery which surrounded the disappearance of the painting that made the case so celebrated. For a quarter of a century it was absolutely lost to the world. People wondered whether it was still in existence, and just as they became sure that it had been destroyed, it was announced that it had been located again. Time after time there were rumors it had been found, but the Gainsborough did not reappear until Adam Worth was ready.

To those who were not on the inside there was certainly something strangely baffling about the whole affair. The portrait in question was that of Georgianna, Duchess of Devonshire, recognized as one of Gainsborough's masterpieces.

Aside from its value as a wonderful example of the painter's art, it had the added attraction of being the best representation of one of the most beautiful and fascinating women in England during the latter half of the 18th century. The subject, daughter of John, Earl Spencer, and wife of William, fifth Duke of Devonshire, was popularly known as the "Electioneering Duchess" from the fact that at times she aided her husband when he stood for election, and had no scruple in kissing the butcher, the baker, and the cabinet-maker, if she thought she could thus gain votes.

Just before the picture was stolen, in the late seventies, it had been purchased by Messrs. Agnew, art dealers, at an auction in the rooms of Christie & Manson, London. The price paid was 10,500 guineas, and the final sale was made only after spirited bidding in which the agent of the Duke of Devonshire took a leading part.

Immediately after they had acquired it, Messrs. Agnew placed it on exhibition in their private gallery at 59 Bond street, London. The large sum that had been paid for it, the publicity that had resulted and the undoubted merit of the painting itself soon drew thousands to the gallery.

Cousins, the engraver, was commissioned to make copies of the picture, and the general interest, is shown by the fact that some 12,000 guineas had already been subscribed for the first proofs. In fact the picture was the fad of the hour.

Then suddenly one morning, members of the Agnew firm entered the gallery and found only an empty frame. The portrait had been cut away and there remained not the slightest clue as to how the thing had been accomplished. The gallery was guarded by a watchman, but he had charge also of several stores in the vicinity, and of course could not guard the picture all the time. The janitor slept on the premises.

When the theft was announced there was a great stir. There seemed to be no way of explaining it. The policeman on the beat, the watchman, the janitor, all said they had seen no suspicious persons about. There was nothing to show how the thief had entered and left the building. All sorts of theories were advanced, but no satisfactory solution was forthcoming. It was not until many years later that any light was thrown upon the mystery.

Naturally all sorts of stories have been told about the case. There was one that said the job was put up by Charlie Becker, "The Dutchman," leader of a gang of forgers, who was said to have secured the picture in order to force the Agnews to go bonds for a pal who had been arrested in

France and brought back to England. It is true that Worth knew Becker, but forgery was never Adam's line, and in his conversations with me he never mentioned Becker or Becker's friends.

"Little Joe" Elliott, another forger of note, has also been mentioned in connection with the robbery. Years after the theft he is said to have offered to secure the return of the picture provided he was released from jail in New York state. He was then serving time for a $64,000 forgery. The police refused to take any action in regard to his offer.

Personally I do not believe that Elliott had anything to do with the matter. I know of course that he and Worth were together in a $200,000 diamond robbery in Paris, but Worth never mentioned "Little Joe's" name when we talked of the Gainsborough picture.

I knew "Little Joe" well. Indeed, I was one of his few friends after he was freed from prison and I was alone with him at the time of his last illness and death in New York City. Elliott never said anything about the Gainsborough theft.

I mention these stories because they have been frequently accepted as the true ones. The version I am about to give is what I gleaned from Worth while working with him in the sale of the Kimberley diamonds.

Worth had gone to London immediately after the plundering of the Boylston Bank in Boston late in the year 1869. His share of the loot amounted to some $150,000 in bonds which he promptly sold in Frankfort.

It is sometimes forgotten that Adam was probably the most notable crook that Boston ever produced. He was so long identified with gigantic robberies in other parts of the world that his beginnings are often completely lost sight of. It was in Boston, however, that he was first initiated into crime and it was knowledge of the city that made the Boylston bank affair so successful.

The son of a Jewish banker in Woburn, his early waywardness led his family to turn him out and thereafter he became a boy of the streets in this city. He sold papers, blacked boots, and engaged in petty stealing whenever chance favored him.

Later he went to New York, where he became a thief. His wonderful ability to organize soon gave him prominence there in a small way, but it was the robbery of the Boylston Bank in Boston which made his reputation among his associates and gave him his first really large haul.

From the time he established himself in England, he became gradually more and more a leader in the enormous robberies which startled the British police and the police of the Continent. Worth was by no means a common crook. He could play the part of the gentleman to perfection and, when he wanted to, could assume the most attractive manners and address that would deceive the most suspicious.

With his $150,000 he set up an elaborate establishment in London, posing as a wealthy American and while he was in funds gave a fine exhibition of all that "high life" means. Nor did he confine himself to the British capital. He was equally familiar with Paris and was associated in that city with his old pal in the Boylston Bank Affair, "Piano Charlie" Bullard, and the latter's beautiful wife. Later he bought out Bullard's notorious American café and there engineered the $200,000 diamond robbery which was only second in importance to that of the famous Kimberley gems.

Between the time of the Gainsborough theft and the Boylston Bank robbery a number of years had elapsed, years in which Adam made much money and spent it as easily as he acquired it. That decade of his life is as full of incident as a novel, but it is not my intention of going into details here.

There was no need for Worth to save money, for he knew that when he had spent what he had, he could easily steal more. Indeed, between his various operations, he amused himself with all the zest and ease of a millionaire. It was only when he saw his funds becoming low that he became unusually active.

One of the lean periods set in during the late seventies and it was to restock his treasury that he turned his attention to the Kimberley diamonds. That trick and the Gainsborough affair are intimately associated because it was to secure funds to finance the South African scheme that he turned his attention to the portrait.

With Charlie St. Clair he had gone to Port Elizabeth, South Africa, and made the preliminary plans for looting the mails containing the Kimberley stones. He then returned to England to secure funds to enable him to put the deal through.

He had his campaign all mapped out, but needed $15,000, and it was to secure this that he went after the Gainsborough. Returning from South Africa to London, he made a flying trip to America and then back to England again.

Soon after he arrived he found all London talking about the "Electioneering Duchess," and naturally his curiosity was excited. Clad in the conventional costume of an English gentleman, he sauntered into the Agnew gallery. He admired the picture, but was more pleased to note hoe easily the place could be broken into by a burglar of any skill.

On the spur of the moment he decided that he wanted the picture, although he was somewhat puzzled to determine just how he could turn it into cash. He needed $15,000 badly, however, for his South African project, and was willing to take the chance that the Agnews would pay heavily for the return of the painting.

As Worth told the story to me, he only had one associate in what followed. That was Jack Phillips, an English crook. I never knew Phillips well, but he had the reputation of being better supplied with brawn than brain. He was a huge, hulking chap well up to six feet in height and broad in proportion.

I could never discover that Phillips played a part much superior to that of a stepladder in the Gainsborough theft. Adam had made a careful survey of the place and knew just what he intended to do.

It was a black and foggy night when he undertook the job. The Agnew gallery was located on the first floor above the street, and over the store below were some iron supports used for spreading an awning.

Worth's plan was daringly simple. It was a bit of burglary that did not demand any great show of skill. The chief danger lay in the fact that he planned to go in from the open street.

When Phillips and he had reached the front of the Agnew place, Worth, who was a small man, jumped easily on the back of his big companion, stepped on his shoulders, reached up and grabbed the awning supports and was on the window ledge in a minute.

The sash offered no difficulty and Worth found himself in the unlighted gallery. From his previous visit he knew the arrangement of the room and no trouble in finding the portrait he sought. A few deft strokes of a sharp knife were sufficient to give him his booty.

Worth understood something about pictures and was careful not to injure the painting in cutting, nor to crack the paint especially on the face in rolling it up. This care showed when the portrait was later returned in excellent condition.

Worth remained in the gallery only a few moments and then left the way he came, carefully closing the window behind him. He disturbed nothing and left not a single tell-tale trace behind.

The affair, however, was by no means over with the securing of the picture. There yet remained the chief difficulty of turning it into coin. Phillips and other friends of Worth's regarded the theft as one that was likely to produce very slim financial results and might bring no end of trouble owing to the furor it had aroused all over England. It looked to them like a good deal of elephant on Worth's hands.

Worth was hard to convince at the start, and with his accustomed shrewdness he began to devise ways and means of getting it back to the owners. He had been more familiar with American methods and was not then aware of how far British conservatism might go.

In one way or another he got in touch with the solicitors of Messrs. Agnew and made overtures for the return of the painting provided he was given a substantial reward. He believed that the negotiations could not fail, but a little later was surprised to learn that, much as the owners wanted the picture, they would not buy it back from a thief and thus place themselves in the light of compounding a felony under the law.

There the matter ended for the time being and all business was dropped. Worth secured his money for the South African trip from another source and determined to store away the picture as an investment until better times. Meanwhile Phillips was grumbling and after several arguments in one of which the big man and the little man came to a clinch. Worth paid Phillips $500 for his share in the picture.

In the years directly following the robbery Adam was fortunate in a number of deals which he put through, and when I first saw the portrait he was living the life of a man of wealth in a fine house in London.

There is no need to go into the business that brought us together, the sale of the Kimberley diamonds. Like Worth, I was a man of property at that time, living on my estate on the continent. It happened that I had just been in Italy to get copies of some paintings there and was returning with them when I visited Worth.

In the course of my stay we became more friendly than we had ever been before, and on one occasion when we were speaking of my pictures he mentioned the case in which they were kept. That was a long, narrow tin tube in which the canvases were rolled.

"Something like that," he said, "would be a fine thing for my picture." Of course I had been sufficiently in touch with the doings of the underworld to know that he meant the Gainsborough portrait. I gave him the tin case and as a result he began to tell me the history of the theft.

He had never been able to discover a way of "working it back" to the owners with any profit to himself, and for that reason had to keep the portrait in hiding, a thing that was dangerous and might lead to his detection at any time.

We discussed ways and means for a while and then he said: "I think I have the right idea. I'm about to make some alterations in the basement of the house and I do not see why I should not take care of the picture at the same time."

I thought no more of it until later, when one day he brought me down in the cellar. There we found another man, a workman whom Worth knew he could trust, making some changes in the wall. Into the masonry there had been built a sort of little vault, and when it was done Adam brought out the Duchess and, rolling up the canvas, packed it in the tin tube and placed it in the compartment. While he and I watched, the other man walled it in. That was the last time I saw the picture.

How long it remained in that particular hiding place I do not know, nor did I ever hear just how it traveled about after that. At any rate, in one way or another it came to this country and was ready for delivery in 1901, a full quarter-century later.

It was typical of Worth that he should hold on until he was sure of his price. The manner of finally disposing of it I learned from one of the men most interested in the business. As the seasons passed, Worth's fertile brain was busy on a variety of schemes, and the matter of the portrait did not bother him greatly.

There were, of course, many private agencies interested from time to time in the search for the portrait, but none of the extended investigations brought results. Worth held on to the picture and continued to live in England without being molested.

The end of the 19th century still found him prosperous. He had plenty of money and was very much the gentleman of means. He had always been a great yachtsman and was particularly fond of sailing. It was one of his cruises to Egypt that led to the final return of the painting.

It chanced that at a hotel at Cairo he fell in with "Pat" Sheedy, a "gentleman gambler" of international reputation. Worth had never met his compatriot, but knew him well by reputation, for Sheedy had a wide acquaintance among the wealthier class of crooks. When the pair became better acquainted, Adam did not hesitate to broach the subject of the Gainsborough portrait.

Sheedy, who was something of an amateur in art and kept tabs on that sort of thing, saw at once a chance for a scoop. He was a friend of William A. Pinkerton and suggested to Worth that the most effective way of "working back" the Stolen Duchess was to place the matter in the hands of Pinkerton.

Sheedy was given authority to open up the negotiation at once and returned to America, where he laid the matter before the noted detective. I have been informed that the thing that made the successful outcome possible was the death of Queen Victoria.

It seems that the warrants issued at the time the Gainsborough was stolen were in the name of the Queen. Before further action could be taken new warrants would have to be made out in the name of King Edward and new evidence gathered. If the transaction went through before the new warrants appeared, it was possible to negotiate the return of the portrait without being liable to the penalties of compounding a felony.

However that may be, Pinkerton at once got in touch with C. Moreland Agnew, son of the original purchaser, by cable. Agnew cabled £100 to cover expenses and Pinkerton replied with a brief cablegram that read: "One hundred pounds only cigarette money. Send £500."

After that the business was begun in earnest. Mr. Agnew sailed for this country and went at once to Chicago, where the deal was closed. Sheedy got the portrait from Worth and turned it over to Pinkerton.

The portrait was taken to Agnew's hotel and he saw at a glance that it was genuine and in excellent condition. It had been agreed that a reward of $20,000 should be paid, and the money was turned over at once. Pinkerton refused absolutely to take any share of the reward from either party in the transaction and was content with the usual charges for work of that delicate nature. Later he was given an excellent copy of the portrait by Mr. Agnew.

Agnew returned with the picture to London and was able to fit it to its original frame. It was sold later to J. Pierpont Morgan for a sum quoted at $150,000.

2 HOW ADAM WORTH STOLE THE KIMBERLEY DIAMONDS

In all the long list of sensational robberies in which that famous Boston crook, Adam Worth, was the central figure there is none that exceeds in skill and daring the theft of the Kimberley diamonds at Port Elizabeth, South Africa in 1881. The loot in that single instance consisted of uncut stones, jewels in the rough, valued at $450,000.

So carefully and patiently had the crime been planned that Worth got away unmolested, returned to London, where he made his headquarters then, and sold his booty in a market comparatively open to dealers from Holland. It was not until long afterwards that he was even suspected of having a share in the affair.

I knew Worth intimately for a number of years, was associated with him on several occasions and in this particular case was his agent in the disposal of the gems. Noted thief-takers have called him the most remarkable criminal of his time. At the very least I must admit that he was one of the most remarkable.

The passing seasons have somewhat dimmed his memory, even among those who make a study of the underworld, and with the general public his deeds, or misdeeds, have been almost wholly forgotten. I do not intend here to give a history of his career. It may be well, however, to call attention to the fact that he was the son of an obscure baker in one of the towns about Boston, that he spent his boyhood in this city, a street urchin, and later drifted into crime as a petty thief and bounty jumper during the civil war.

In later years he became the leader in criminal operations of various kinds, which netted somewhere in the vicinity of $4,000,000. He was the chief of the band which plundered the Boylston Bank in this city, he stole single-handed the Gainsborough portrait of the Duchess of Devonshire and had a hand in a number of other robberies of scarcely less importance. For years he lived in England, posing as a wealthy American, and thwarted all the attempts of the police of Great Britain to bring him to book.

There have been numberless accounts of the Kimberley diamond case, the most celebrated of its sort, but the one I'm about to give is the only true narrative. I had it from the lips of Adam Worth himself at the time when the incidents were still fresh in his mind.

As a matter of fact, I became interested in the robbery before it was committed. In the year 1880 I was living on my estate on the continent, very much the gentleman and rich proprietor. I had amassed a fortune in the United States by a series of successful bank burglaries and had settled down to live respectably. My reputation as a skilled safe-breaker still clung to me, however.

That reputation was responsible for bringing me in touch with Worth. One day I received an urgent letter from my confidential business agent in New York asking me to communicate with Worth, who was then living in

London. I was informed that the matter was one of importance and likely to prove profitable.

As a result there was some correspondence between Worth and me, and the upshot of it was a meeting at the Hotel Kaiserhof in Frankfort, Germany. It was then that Adam broached the subject of diamond robbery and asked me to undertake the job with him.

He told me that most of the preliminaries had already been arranged and even showed me the key of the safe from which the diamonds were to be taken. He had the scheme worked out to the last details, for crime with him was a business and conducted with all business caution. The plan however, had very serious difficulties, chiefly because it called for the delaying either of a Royal Mail coach or a Royal Mail steamer, no light undertaking even in those days.

As it happened, I was pretty well content to live as I had been living. I had plenty of money, was engaged in a delicate business deal, and wanted to continue "on the square" if I could. I refused all Worth's offers and heard no more from him for nearly a year.

Then in 1881 I received another letter from Worth requesting me to come at once to London. I went without delay and there he told me that he had turned the diamond trick without my aid and wanted some clever and trustworthy man to undertake the sale of the gems. We came to terms when Worth made a verbal agreement that he would give me a bonus of $25,000 and pay all my expenses. He then showed me a heap of diamonds big enough to fill a high silk hat.

We hired an office in High Holborn, London, furnished it in proper style and installed a clerk. I then went to Holland and got in touch with a number of diamond cutters. The buyers came from week to week for a few months until all the stones had been sold.

It was during this time that Worth told me the story of the robbery, bit by bit, and the different incidents were repeated so often that they have remained as clear in my mind as when Worth first recounted them.

It was in the year 1878 that he turned his attention to South Africa. The discovery of the diamond fields at Kimberley had started a mining fever, and scores of small prospectors rushed to the region. It occurred to Worth that the place was bound to yield him a profit in one way or another.

Accordingly, he and his partner, Charlie St. Clair, purchased a new power steam engine and other mining implements in New York and boarded the next vessel for Port Elizabeth. As Worth told me the tale, he had the actual intention of doing some real mining. He and St. Clair set out at once for Kimberley and set up their plant.

The pair figured that they would be insured against loss, for if they found no diamonds of their own, they could at least steal some of those that their more successful neighbors unearthed. They were not long in discovering that they were not cut out for miners, and that hard work did not seem suitable to their constitutions.

They began operations by filching some stones from neighboring miners, but soon saw that they were under suspicion, and, fearing the consequences, sold out their plant and returned to Port Elizabeth. It was just before this that Worth's busy brain caught the stupendous idea of stealing the Kimberley output in transit.

At that time a railroad was under construction from Port Elizabeth into the interior, but still fell short of Kimberley by some 400 miles. To make up for this deficiency the government had established a line of mail coaches from Kimberley to the nearest station on the railroad. This led to a practice by the owners of the various mining claims of sending their uncut stones by mail to London.

Once every two weeks a mail steamer called at Port Elizabeth to pick up the mail from Kimberley and other sections. For that reason the dispatching of the mail bags containing the diamonds for London was so timed that the mail coach could meet a train that would bring the mail to Port Elizabeth on the exact day on which the mail steamer called. In that way the diamonds were assured an unbroken journey from Kimberley to London.

Worth was never a man given to rough work. He preferred to make his mind take the place of physical force. To a criminal of his experience it was plain that the only way to get at the diamonds without a violent hold-up was to make them stop over somewhere on the route.

In order to make a theft anything like successful, however, the robbers would have to know the exact place of that stopover some days ahead of time so that they could make the robbery easy and sure.

Worth saw that he had the choice of two plans. He would either have to delay the Kimberley mail coach so that it could not meet the train for Port Elizabeth, or he would have to cause some accident to happen to the Royal Mail steamer so that it could not make Port Elizabeth on the day of its schedule.

In either case he figured that the diamonds would lie over for a night or for a number of nights at Port Elizabeth and that he could then make some plan by which they could be stolen without resorting to dangerous methods.

Worth and St. Clair went to work at once on the details of their project. They timed their departure from Kimberley so as to travel by the mail coach which carried the diamonds in order to keep a tally on everything that happened. The route ran in a southerly direction out of Kimberley to the Orange river at Hopetown, some 100 miles distant. There the coach was ferried across the river on a flatboat or pontoon and then resumed its journey to the nearest railroad station some 300 miles further on.

The road which the coach traveled was only sparsely settled by Boer plantations and was dotted at considerable distances by stations where the coach horses were changed. Worth and St. Clair stuck to the diamond bags all through the trip, watched them as they were put on the train and finally observed the transfer from the train to the steamer which was lying at the dock ready to sail for England.

The two conspirators remained in Port Elizabeth for some time, taking a room at the best hotel and making themselves friendly with the residents. All the while they were looking over the ground carefully. After considerable study they decided that the best place to attempt the robbery was in Port Elizabeth itself.

Worth thought at the time that the best way to put through the scheme was to delay the mail steamer. He understood that if the ship did not arrive until a day or two later than usual that would be no reason for delaying the sending of the Kimberley diamonds.

He figured that the two mail bags which contained the stones would come through on the regular train and, when it was found that the steamer would not arrive, would be deposited in the post office in Port Elizabeth to await the arrival later.

Worth planned to prepare the post office in advance so that the burglary would not be too hard a job for one man, and then decided that the second man should be sent to Cape Town, 300 miles further down the coast, to board the steamer. During the run to Port Elizabeth he considered that it would be an easy matter for the second man to put some fine-ground emery into the oil cups of the bearings of the engine. That, of course, would heat the journals so effectively that the engine would have to be stopped for repairs and the steamer delayed possibly for several days.

In the meantime, the first man would wait in Port Elizabeth for the arrival of the diamonds, and when the Kimberley mail bags were deposited in the post office for the night it would be his share of the scheme to force an entrance, rifle the mail bags, and get away with the booty.

Naturally the first thing to do was to make the burglary end of the plan sure. This was exactly in Worth's line. It was a business that he understood very well. He went at once to the post office and discovered that all valuables were kept in a large iron safe of English make which was secured by a Chubb lock, the best lock in use at that time in England.

Worth realized that what he needed most was a duplicate of the postmaster's key. With that in view he and St. Clair made the acquaintance of that official, who proved to be an affable fellow and convivial soul.

During the two weeks that they remained in Port Elizabeth between steamers, they were frequently in the postmaster's company and were soon on the best of terms with him. For so clever a crook as Worth it was not difficult to turn the conversation to keys, and when he was inspecting the key of the post office safe to take an impression of it on a bit of wax concealed in his palm.

That much accomplished, Worth decided to go back to England. When the next mail steamer arrived, he and St. Clair departed, receiving a cordial send-off from their friend the postmaster. In London they had several keys made from the wax impression. This was done because they wanted to be sure that some one of the false keys would fit. The Chubb lock people had made the claim that no key that would work could be made fine enough to be of any value from a wax impression.

Worth wanted to go back to South Africa at once, but found that he did not have money enough to finance the robbery so as to make it absolutely safe. During the years 1879 and 1880 business seemed pretty slack for crooks in England, and Worth did not make any considerable haul.

It was not until an English gang of crooks invited him to take part in the robbery of an express car attached to the Calais Paris train that he secured the stake he needed. Worth's share in that affair amounted to about $40,000. After that he was prepared to undertake the Kimberley robbery without fear.

Worth then arranged that Charlie St. Clair should go with his wife to South Africa on a pleasure trip and pay an incidental visit to the postmaster at Port Elizabeth with a view of finding out whether any of the false keys fitted the safe. St. Clair had no trouble in getting to the safe and found that the keys worked to perfection. He then took the next steamer back to England and reported progress to Worth.

All was now in readiness for the attempt. It had been understood that Worth was to commit the actual robbery, and that St. Clair was to board the Royal Mail steamer and cause the engines to break down on the trip between Cape Town and Port Elizabeth.

At the last minute, however, St. Clair lost his courage and began to back water. He was afraid to take the chance of tampering with the steamer's engine and refused absolutely to agree to Worth's plan. It was then that Adam made his appeal to me to help him out. There, too, as I have stated, he met with disappointment.

Worth was not a man easily baffled. As soon as he saw he could not count on St. Clair in his original plan, he began at once to scheme out an alternative. He gave up on the idea of delaying the steamer altogether and turned his attention at once to the mail coach.

He knew that the delaying of the coach was by no means as sure as the delaying of the steamer, for if the coach were stopped only a limited time, it was perfectly possible that the steamer might be held for a time at Port Elizabeth.

Still, he was willing to try his luck. In order to carry out the robbery, he first sent a married couple, relatives of his, to Port Elizabeth. These people were to hire a furnished house and it was arranged that he should go to them and remain under cover so that he would not have to meet people he had known during his previous stay at the town.

When the wet season had arrived in 1881 Worth arrived in Port Elizabeth by steamer bringing with him the false key of the post office safe and another which fitted the post office door.

He had chosen the wet season for an excellent reason. During the dry months, as he was well aware, the Orange river is a low and not very formidable stream, but once the rains have set in in good earnest it becomes a torrent with considerable overflow.

It was his idea to halt the coach at that point on the north side of the river. It arrived at the north bank usually in the morning, was immediately ferried across to a station on the opposite shore where the horses were changed and then resumed its long journey to meet the railroad.

Worth's scheme was simple and effective. On the night before the arrival of the coach which carried the diamonds he decided to cut the steel wire cable upon which the ferry was operated by means of pulleys. He figured that the flatboat, once cast adrift, would be caught by the turbulent current and driven down stream for many miles.

If his maneuver was successful, it would take considerable time to recover the pontoon and in the meantime the mail steamer would have left Port Elizabeth. Thus the gems would lie over at the Port Elizabeth post office until the next steamer two weeks later.

Everything fell out as Worth had anticipated. During the weeks before the date of the robbery he had instructed his relative to purchase a good team of horses and a buckboard. The rig was taken down to the last station on the railroad, and there Worth took charge of it, sending his relative back to Port Elizabeth.

He drove on at his leisure through the splendid country, and at last arrived at the relay station on the south side of the river the night before the Kimberley coach was due. At about 11 o'clock when everybody was asleep he stole out of the station, cut the wire cable with a hatchet and sent the flatboat spinning down the river at a rapid rate. There was only one rowboat the station, and after smashing a hole in the bottom of this he sent it off into midstream to sink.

On the following morning the bugle of the coach was heard sounding on the opposite bank, but when the station people came to look for their ferry it was nowhere to be seen. The coach was effectively held up and a search was instituted for the runway flatboat. It was finally picked up some 16 miles below, and before it was towed back two full days had elapsed.

Nobody suspected Worth, but a kaffir boy, who had been discharged a few days before, was held responsible for the mischief and beaten unmercifully by the people of the station.

As soon as Worth saw that his activities had been successful at the Orange river, he drove off again to the railroad and left his horses and buckboard with a Boer planter to be kept until he should call for them. He continued on to Port Elizabeth by train.

There he found that everything had gone as he had hoped. The mail coach men had telegraphed ahead to explain the delay, but the captain of the mail steamer refused to lay by for the arrival of the mail and started at once for England.

Two days later the Kimberley mail bags with $450,000 in diamonds arrived in Port Elizabeth. There was nothing to do but remove the stones to the post office to remain until the next steamer arrived 12 days later.

Worth had plenty of time to act and after waiting a few nights decided to make an attempt on the post office. With the key which he had already prepared he opened the door of the building at 10 o'clock in the evening and walked in.

To his great surprise he found the safe door standing wide open and the two enormously valuable mailbags piled carelessly beside the safe. It was something of a shock to Worth, for he had waited two years to turn a trick which might have been put through by an amateur burglar. The keys with which he had taken so much trouble were not needed at all.

There was one thing which Worth had overlooked, however, and it came near to setting all his preparations at naught. The postmaster lived just above the office, and in order to reach his rooms he had to pass through the lower office and up a stairway which overlooked the office room.

Just as Worth was in the act of cutting open the diamond bags he heard the street door open and the step of the postmaster crossing the room. While the robber crouched in the darkness, expecting detection at any moment, the postmaster walked across to the stairway and went upstairs. He was so accustomed to the place that he did not strike a light, and so careless that he did not give an eye to the treasure that he was supposed to guard.

When at last Worth was satisfied that his friends was asleep, he began to work on the bags. Inside he found a number of small tin boxes done up in wrappers with string and sealing wax, indicating that there had been numerous individual senders of diamonds.

Without stopping to think, the thief opened all of these packages on the spot and poured the contents promiscuously in a cloth bag which he had brought with him. That was a bad error of judgment which caused him considerable trouble, work, and loss later on. Naturally most of the shippers had sorted their stones according to the different grades and had divided them into separate packages. By mixing them thus together he jumbled the grades into one big heap.

To sort these rough diamonds again would require the services of a person made expert by long experience. Worth told me that if he had not mixed the stones he have sold the lot for from $40,000 to $50,000 more than he actually received.

He got every stone of the whole consignment with the exception of one large diamond which had rolled under a pile of letters and was found next day by the police. He then left the office, locking the door carefully behind him and went to his quarters to prepare for a safe getaway.

The next morning the theft was discovered. The postmaster was suspected at once and closely questioned by the police. The result was the unearthing of one of the strangest bits of circumstantial evidence that has ever come to my attention.

It happened that when the postmaster's apartments and belongings were searched the officers found in a pocket of the postmaster's coat a stolen letter. The text showed that the writer had sent a £5 Bank of England note to friends at home and that the postmaster had taken this money for his own use. The sender, by chance, had taken the number of the note so that the case was clear against the postmaster.

This peculiar circumstance was accepted by the community as proof that the postmaster must have had a hand in the larger theft. He was placed on trial later, but for want of conclusive evidence on the burglary count was sentenced to five years in prison on the charge of stealing letters from the mail.

After separating the larger stones and those of fine appearance from the rest, Worth stowed them away in the belts about his body, leaving the rest with his relative. He took a train up country, got his horses and buckboard from the Boer planter with whom he had left them and started out on a drive of some 300 miles across the country, then only slightly settled by Boer farmers, to Port Natal, near the town of Durban. He took his time on the journey, stopping from time to time at the various Boer plantations.

Once arrived at Port Natal he sold his outfit and boarded a steamer for Cape Town. There he took another steamer bound for England by way of the Red sea and the Suez canal. On the ship he met a man whom he had known in the Kimberley diamond fields in other years, and, fearing that some complication might arise he went ashore at Aden and picked up a sailing vessel on which he continued his journey to England.

His relative remained in Port Elizabeth for some months, and then when he was sure that he was not under suspicion, took the steamer for England with his wife. They brought with them the rest of the diamonds.

It was then I was called in to help in the disposing of the plunder. The grading of the stones, which was done at best imperfectly, was a long and tedious job, and there were doubtless many stones without a flaw and of pure water which remained mixed in with the poorer lots. This fact did not escape the attention of the expert diamond cutters from the Continent and probably accounts for the rapidity with which the diamonds were sold.

Although the whole lot was valued at $450,000, Worth realized only $350,000 in actual cash. Of this sum he kept $250,000, to his relative he gave $60,000 and to his former partner, Charlie St. Clair, $10,000. As he had agreed, he gave me $25,000 for acting as his broker in the sale. His actual expenses he figured at $5000.

It is curious that Worth, who was so successful in this particular case, was baffled in a lesser diamond robbery only a short time before. The two affairs form a part of the same series of events, for the unsuccessful attempt was designed to furnish funds for the Kimberley diamond robbery.

The thing occurred while Worth and St. Clair were waiting in London after their first trip to South Africa. Worth was using every means to raise some funds and it occurred to him at last that it might be a good plan to operate upon some of the diamond dealers to whom the Kimberley miners shipped their gems.

With this end in view Worth and St. Clair, both of whom were of gentlemanly appearance and manners, made the acquaintance of a diamond dealer named Proctor. They had learned that he was in the habit of receiving some $50,000 in diamonds from Kimberley every second week.

Worth found out the day that the diamonds usually arrived and determined to have a try at Proctor's safe. In the meantime the confederates became quite friendly with Proctor. What they needed was a duplicate of his safe key.

One day when Worth and St. Clair met Proctor he told them that he was about to take a Turkish bath and the other two me saw immediately that this might give them their desired opportunity. They decided to go with him and when they reached the bath Worth noticed that Proctor did not leave his keys with his other valuables at the desk.

While the men were in the bath St. Clair remained with Proctor, while Worth made an excuse to leave them for a minute. He stepped out into the dressing room, found Proctor's clothes and taking his keys from his pocket, made a wax impression of them. He then restored them and rejoined his companions.

The safe key was of a complicated pattern and when it had been made Worth took the precaution to slip into Proctor's office and try it in the safe. It worked perfectly and nothing remained but to wait for the day on which the diamonds arrived.

Worth concealed himself in the building in which offices were located. That night he forced the office door, went to the safe, but when he opened it, was surprised and chagrined to find nothing of value there. As luck would have it, the steamer which usually brought the diamonds brought no consignment on that particular date. Worth closed and locked the safe door and left.

When Proctor arrived the next day he found that his door had been tampered with, but saw no other signs of an attempt at burglary. The affair remained a mystery to the London police and this is probably the first time that any explanation of the case has been made.

The result, however, was that Proctor watched his diamonds so closely thereafter that Worth never made another visit to the place.

3 MARK SHINBORN'S STORY OF THE CONCORD BANK ROBBERY

From the point of view of an expert bank burglar the robbery of the Concord Bank at Concord, Mass., in 1865, is perhaps as queer a case as any in the records of New England crime. Langdon W. Moore, who was the prime mover in the affair, secured some $300,000, and on account of the booty gained a reputation as a crook of the first class. How far he deserved it may be gathered from the story I am going to tell.

To me, as a safe-breaker of long experience, there has always been a semi-humorous side to the whole series of events, and I am frank to say at the outset that I can recall no other operation which was at once so bungling and so successful.

At that time, as a matter of fact, Moore was little better than an amateur. He spent months in carrying out a job which I could have done easily in a day or two at the most. I often smile when I think of the crude methods he used and the huge deal of useless labor and scheming he expended. Still, he got what he went after in the end, and that was about all the public cared for.

Although I never worked with Moore, I knew him for nearly half a century. I first met him back in 1862 in New York City. He was then known as Charlie Adams, was backing a faro game on Houston street, and was the close friend of a number of counterfeiters and other crooks. In years after, I heard of his doings from time to time, but did not become intimate with him until he was an old man.

For several years before he died, in 1911, he had lived in retirement on a farm about two miles from the town of West Swanzey, N.H. and there I visited him frequently and gossiped with him about old times. It was from these conversations that I learned the true facts of the Concord Bank break.

Curiously enough, I had good reason to be interested in the Concord Bank because I had planned to plunder it myself just previous to the time that Moore worked out his scheme. Anyone who cares to look up my record will find that I was arrested in April, 1865, charged with the robbery of the Walpole Bank at Walpole, N.H.

I had turned that trick easily enough and was about to attack the bank at Keene, N.H., when the police caught me at my farm in Saratoga. The detectives found in my possession keys half-made from wax impressions which would fit the Keene institution. That fact was afterwards brought against me.

What the detectives did not know was that the Concord Bank was third on my list, and if I had remained free I would have gone after it when I had cleaned up my work at Keene. As it turned out, my arrest gave Moore free play.

I ought to explain that all during the civil war and immediately after it the country was flooded with counterfeit paper money which was put in circulation by a band of counterfeiters in New York City. The circulation of these bad bills made necessary the employment of a system of confederates in scores of communities in the East. Many of the workers, although supposed to be respectable citizens, were in reality spies, and in addition to passing the counterfeits kept the New York underworld informed as to likely prospects for burglaries.

It was from the counterfeiters that I obtained my information as to the Concord Bank, and it was from the same source that Moore got his tip. The job looked like a simple and attractive one. As both Moore and I were told, the cashier of the bank went home to his dinner every day at noon and did not return again to the bank until an hour and a half or two hours had passed.

He had been watched by the counterfeiter's spy, and it was known that before leaving he either put the money chest, without stopping to lock it, inside the bank vault, or, if he did lock it, put the key of the box on the shelf inside the vault.

After that he locked the doors of the vault with several keys and then placed the vault keys in a drawer under the bank counter. The problem was almost absurdly easy to a crook of any skill. All that was absolutely necessary was to get the key of the outer door of the bank. All the other keys lay ready to hand and could be taken without effort.

There were several ways that I could have carried out the robbery. The simplest, of course, would be to get an impression of the street door key and go in at noon and open the vault and money chest with the cashier's keys.

The method I had used in a score of burglaries would have held good there. All I had to do was find out where the cashier lived, force an entrance into his house at night, go to his room and take the keys. I could then either go at once to the bank and rob it or I could take impressions of the keys in wax, make duplicates, and attack the bank at my leisure.

The simplest, although the most dangerous, method of all, however, would have been to take a single impression of the key to the door of the bank and then go at noon and carry the whole thing through without any bother. The cashier would never suspect that there was a duplicate of his door key until after the place had been plundered.

I have seldom heard of a robbery which offered fewer complications. I should have done it all alone and in short order. With Moore the case was different, for he had been up to that time only a confidence man and sport. He knew next to nothing about burglary, and it was only natural that the one simple lock on the door of the bank should loom up to him like a stupendous puzzle. It always makes me chuckle to think of it.

My informant in the Concord Bank matter was a weighty citizen of the community, who transacted not a little business with the bank, and was only incidentally an ally of the false money men. He liked the work I had done at Walpole, and kept an eye on the cashier at Concord for me. He was in constant communications with me between November, 1864, when I "got" the Walpole Bank, and April, 1865, when I was arrested.

When I was behind the bars he met Langdon Moore, with whom he had some dealings in counterfeits, and mentioned the Concord Bank to him. Moore at that time was living on a farm in Natick, some 12 miles distant. He had purchased the place early in 1864 and made it his headquarters for circulating and selling false bills, a business in which he was extensively engaged.

One of his closest pals was Harry Howard, a passer of counterfeit money. Howard was no more a burglar than Moore. He was never a very clever crook, and was killed ten years later in New York City by a burglar, who believed Moore had "squealed." The burglar was never brought to justice.

As soon as he heard of the large amount of plunder that he might get from the Concord Bank, Moore was fired with an ambition to become a bank smasher, an told his schemes to Howard. The latter was only too willing to help.

Neither man had any idea of "sneaking," an art in itself which comes only after long practice, and for that reason it never occurred to the pair to go to the cashier's house and steal his keys.

Moore made a scouting visit to the bank when the cashier opened up one day after dinner. He observed that the casher on entering left his key in the street door and went upstairs to open up the banking rooms without returning to get the door key until later.

The prospective burglar noted that the door to the banking rooms was of the simplest construction and could be readily picked even by an amateur by means of a skeleton key, but that the lock on the front door was one of the strongest and best makes of the time.

Moore watched the cashier closely and saw him take the vault keys from the drawer under the counter. He could not make out, however, where the key to the strongbox was kept, and left that detail for a future visit.

A few days later Moore and Howard drove to the bank again from Natick and waited until the cashier returned from his dinner. He went through the same routine as before, leaving the street door key in the lock. Moore went upstairs with him while Howard remained below.

Moore was rewarded for his vigilance by seeing the key of the money chest taken from a shelf inside the vault, and concluded that if he could make sure of the outer door, the rest would be comparatively easy. The cashier had managed his keys just as he had on the first visit, so that they spy concluded that it was his regular habit to open his vault and box in just that same way every day.

In order to give his visit a businesslike look, Moore opened negotiations with the banker for the purchase of several thousand dollars' worth of 7-30 U.S. government bonds. The banker said that he did not have any in hand, but if Moore would call at a stated date in the future there would be a lot to the value of $70,000, which had already been ordered.

In the meantime Howard had been busy below. Watching his opportunity, he took out the street door key, made an impression of it in wax and then returned it to the lock. Moore then left the bank and the pair drove back to Natick to make duplicates of the key.

That would not have been difficult for anyone who knew the intricacies of locks and safes, but to Moore and Howard, who were woefully ignorant, it was a trying job. At last their keys were completed and they returned again to the bank, but when they fitted their keys into the lock they found that not a single one would work.

Nearly 50 years later Moore explained this trouble to me at West Swanzey, and in a few moments I told him where his error lay in making the keys from the impression. I mention that point simply to show the difference between an expert burglar and one who thinks himself capable.

Thus these two embryo cracksmen found themselves still face to face with the same old problem, and set about trying to solve it in another way. They were convinced that the trick must be turned in the broad daylight on the principal street of the town. They knew that the keys were not in the bank at night, and for that reason rough methods of breaking the door with crowbars and saws would be of no value. They were afraid to break into the cashier's house.

Moore, in spite of his inexperience, was a man od ready resource. He followed a plan which I once used myself with success. He decided that he must fix the door in some other way. Accordingly, he and Howard went to the bank at night with a ladder.

Howard entered the building through a second-story window and then came down to tackle the street door from the inside. Moore remained outside, and, after concealing the ladder, stayed on post to warn his confederate of any danger.

Howard went to work at once in an attempt to remove the lock, with the idea of finding what there was in it that prevented the false keys from working. And just here I want to say that when Moore related that incident to me I was simply disgusted that any man who thought himself a bank burglar should do anything so foolish. As I told him, it reminded me of a child trying to open a watch to see what made it tick.

As a result of his learned investigations, Howard discovered that the lock was fastened to the door by means of four bolts, each provided with a screw nut. He had a monkey-wrench with him and began to take off the screw nuts.

Here a new trouble arose, for as soon as he tried to force the lock free from the bolts, Moore from his post outside saw the dry paint begin to flake off from the bolt-heads on the outside of the door. He knew that a set of paint-less bolt-heads would be a plain indication that the lock had been tampered with, and ordered Howard to stop. The lock was restored to its place and the two men left the bank again, baffled.

Howard remained in Concord to see whether the cashier noted anything out of the way with the door, and when he discovered that he did not, returned to Natick and reported again to Moore.

Moore understood that before he could work on the lock again, it would have to be removed by somebody else, so any damage to the paint would go unnoticed. He decided to plug the lock from the outside with some obstruction so that the cashier's key would not work. The lock would then have to be taken off and mended, and when the burglars went back again they would not have to bother with flaking paint.

Thus, after a week or so, the burglars drove over again and obstructed the lock very effectually. When the cashier arrived in the morning he could not turn his key, and sent at once for the blacksmith. A committee of citizens gathered and consulted, and finally the blacksmith borrowed the same ladder that Howard had used, entered the bank by the same window and unscrewed the lock from the inside.

The smith had no trouble in removing the plug after the lock had been taken off, and the whole affair was put down as a prank of mischievous boys. When the matter had blown over, the burglars went back to the bank, entered it as before and removed the lock without being afraid of marring the paint. They filed it until one of their false keys would throw the bolt and then put it back.

The preliminary work was now all accomplished; but Moore and Howard still hesitated. It had it that just then a particularly good issue of counterfeit $100 compound interest United states notes came out and the bills looked so attractive to the pair that they gave up the bank job for a while and went off throughout the country passing bad money.

Perhaps it may be well to explain that when the makers of counterfeits put a new bill on the market, they supplied all their patrons as nearly as possible on the same day, so that no one passer could get the jump on his competitors.

Moore and Howard had been informed that the new $100 notes were of the very best quality, and for that reason they did not dare to delay, for fear that someone more enterprising would skim the cream. It was for that reason that they abandoned the bank temporarily.

Toward the end of September in 1865, however, the confederates got back to the farm in Natick and decided that the time had come to loot the Concord Bank. As I calculated, the affair was remarkably easy.

They drove over from the Natick farm just before noon. Everything was quiet. As was the leisurely habit of those days, about everybody had shut up shop and gone home for a noonday dinner. The street was practically deserted.

After watching the cashier leave, Howard brought his rig to a point just opposite the bank, while Moore strolled across the street to the bank building. His false key turned easily, and after closing the door he went upstairs, mastered the lock of the banking room door with a simple skeleton key and then turned his attention to the vault.

As he had expected, he found the keys to the vault in the drawer under the counter. He opened the first vault door and then the second, and once inside was delighted to see the key to the strongbox on a shelf.

He lost no time in rifling the bank of all its treasure in bonds and bills, and having locked the vault and strongbox again went away, taking the keys with him. He did not bother to secure the outer door.

When Moore appeared at the door with a big leather meal bag over his shoulder, Howard drove quickly from the other side of the street, and the pair sped off to Natick without being observed. There they divided the cash, but Moore held on to the securities for future disposal, burying them under the roots of a big tree on his farm. Howard went away almost immediately, and Moore kept moving back and forth between Boston, New York, and the farm at Natick.

When the robbery was discovered the bank officials could make no head nor tail to it. The police of Boston and New York, however, were better informed. They learned that Moore and Howard had been in the vicinity, and knowing that they were agents of the counterfeiters and that the counterfeiters had a hand in most of the big bank jobs, they put two and two together and were pretty well satisfied that the two men could give an explanation of the case if they could be compelled to. Then, too, the story leaked out through the usual underground of police informers.

No clever policeman, however, would undertake to make an arrest on mere suspicion in so important a case as that of the Concord Bank robbery. It takes considerable time to follow down the various leads and get the right kind of evidence.

The detectives on the case knew well that nothing compromising would be found in Moore's possession if he were arrested. They adopted a familiar method of watching Moore's friends and associates, many of whom were known to be passers of false money.

As the police figured it, if some one of these false money men could be caught "dead to rights" with counterfeit money in his hands, he might be willing to inform on Moore on a promise of immunity.

Moore, of course, was aware that the police were after him, and, after spending some time in hiding among his confidential friends, got one of them, a man named Spencer, to hire a house on the New Jersey shore of the Delaware river, about 30 miles from Philadelphia.

Moore dug up his securities at Natick and reburied them on his New Jersey farm, where he intended to stay until the excitement subsided. It was then that Moore made his worst slip. He had engaged his brother to alter the numbers of the stolen bonds and prepared to put the securities on the market through his friends. Of course, the true numbers had been circulated broadcast.

Any experienced crook would have been wise enough to have waited. He would have left the bonds underground for a year at least before trying to dispose of them, and in the meantime they would be bearing constantly accruing interest. Moore, however, was eager to realize on his plunder.

By 1866 the police had arrived close on the trail of Moore. The game they had planned was working well. They had picked out a friend of Moore's, known to the underworld as "Blacksmith Tom," and decided to make him the instrument for Moore's capture.

A job was put up on Tom, who was lured by the tempting bait of counterfeit money. A large bundle was offered to him cheap, and after he had made the purchase and was leaving the place with the false money in his possession he was arrested. Tom was given the choice of going to prison or telling what he knew about Moore.

As a matter of fact he did not know Moore's hiding place, but he did know Moore's confidential agent, and agreed to put the police on the latter's track if guaranteed his freedom. Capt. Jordan of the New York police, who was handling the case, gave Tom his promise, providing Tom would buy some of the stolen securities from Moore's agent and thus tie the robbery definitely to the suspect. There was an added incentive to the work of the police owing to the fact that the bank had offered a reward of $30,000 for the return of the stolen bonds.

"Blacksmith Tom" was set at liberty, under police surveillance and at once got in touch with Moore's agent, who was a well-known livery stable keeper. He made such a tempting offer that the agent went to Moore in New Jersey, got some of the bonds from him, and then returned to meet Tom in New York. He was just in the act of receiving the money and handing over the bond when the police stepped in and arrested him.

The livery man was taken to the station of the old Sixth police precinct and was placed in a small, dark cell known to the crooks at that time as "Jordan's Sweatbox." After some days of this sort of third degree he weakened and told Capt. Jordan where Moore could be found.

Jordan and his men lost no time in getting to Moore's farm. Arriving in two hacks, they jumped out and surrounded the place. Jordan knocked at the front door and was admitted by a maid. As the detectives entered, Moore met them at the head of the stairs, flourishing a large revolver. Jordan decided to halt for a parley, and after considerable debate Moore came down and shook hands all around.

The gist of the parley was this: If Moore had not done the job at Concord, he had nothing to fear. If he had done it, he could make restitution and so arrange matters that he would not have to be taken to Massachusetts. Under either circumstances nothing was to be gained on either side by promiscuous shooting.

All this seemed sensible to Moore, and for that reason he went back willingly enough to New York with Jordan. He was not treated with all the consideration he had expected, however, for once in that station, he, too, was confined to the "Sweatbox" until he should develop a willingness to talk business.

As a final straw they brought the liveryman to his cell, and then Moore knew for the first time that the affair was all over. He decided to make restitution to save both himself and his friend.

Capt. Jordan was well pleased and sent immediately for the Concord Bank people. The negotiations progressed smoothly and it was finally agreed that Moore should give back securities to the value of $200,000, which remained concealed at his farm at Paulsboro, N.J.

The bonds were dug up and turned over to the bank people, who went back to Massachusetts without asking any further punishment for the robber. Jordan received his reward and Moore was discharged from custody by Judge Dowling, who officiated for that purpose in the precinct office of Capt. Jordan.

4 MARK SHINBORN TELLS STORY OF HIS GREATEST PERIL

Even as an old man, when I look back on the events which followed the robbery of the bank at St. Catherine's, Can., in 1868, I can feel my nerves grow taut and my senses thrill strangely with the horror of a night the like of which has fallen the lot of few men. I have faced death in many forms without a qualm of fear, but that experience was enough to bring terror even to the bravest.

I have never sought danger for danger's sake, but the career of an old-time safe robber was necessarily filled with close calls, desperate chances and seemingly impossible escapes. I have seen bullets flying, I have broken jail a number of times, I have eluded capture by seconds, I have prowled about darkened houses, not knowing at what turn fate might cut the thread of my life; in fact, I have played the game without any particular thought of the result.

Those things are part of the routine of a daring crook. The St. Catherine's affair was different. To be sure, the robbery itself had elements of peril, but they were of a kind long familiar and were all in the day's work. What came to pass afterwards was something that happens only once in a lifetime and leaves an impression that is never forgotten.

I have seen many melodramas, old and new, yet nothing in the fiction of the stage has equaled, in my opinion, what befell George White and me. I leave it to the judgment of the reader in the belief that his views will coincide with mine at the close of the chapter.

There we were, two much-sought criminals, escaping with a treasure of some $240,000 from Canada into the United States. Across our path stretched the Niagara river just where the famous falls go tumbling over the precipice. Our only safe way was a bridge which we found closely guarded.

The remaining choice was another bridge, then half finished, which spanned the river a quarter of a mile below the falls. The night was the worst I had ever seen—a raging snow blizzard, with the wind howling a gale. The darkness was inky black.

In the center of the half-completed structure we came upon a chasm, how wide we could not tell. From the finished flooring there jutted a narrow line of 12-inch planks coated with ice. Two hundred feet below rushed the river. We had either to trust ourselves to that light foothold or go back to the Canadian shore and face a long term in the Queen's prison. How we met the difficulty the narrative will show in due time.

It was in the midst of an unusually hard winter in the year 1868, while I was enjoying life in New York City, that George White, alias George Miles, alias George Bliss, approached me with the proposition of robbing the St. Catherine's Bank. He said that he had become interested in the matter through a crook named Jim Griffith and that the job was a simple one.

White and I were associated from time to time in robberies, both before and after this particular affair. He had been a prosperous hotel keeper in Stoneham, Mass., but the authorities in Cheshire county, N.H., had managed to mix him up with the robbery of the Walpole, N.H. Savings Bank, for which I had been responsible, in 1864.

He was placed on trial at Keene in 1865, but the jury disagreed and before his second trial he broke out of jail. After that he went to New York and, out of revenge for the treatment he had received, leagued himself with the crooks of that city and became one of the most successful of American criminals.

White's business training never left him and in his various jobs he was always a stickler for details. Personally he was a man of excellent habits. Wine and women and the various forms of dissipation had no charms for him.

We never regarded each other as partners, although he was at times of great assistance to me in my jobs, as I was to him in his. We worked only for one affair at a time, and after we had divided the spoils, he went on with his own schemes in partnership with other crooks, and I continued to play the part of the lone burglar until I hit upon a robbery which needed more than one man.

On this occasion White was enthusiastic for the proposed robbery. According to the story he told me, the securing of the keys which would make it possible would be easy, for he said that Griffith had already learned that they were left carelessly in the dining room of the cashier's house.

There was a serious difficulty, however, in the fact that a clerk slept in the bank each night, and, according to the plan that White placed before me, it would be necessary not only to steal the vault and safe keys but also to force an entrance into the bank the same night, sneak in upon the clerk while he was asleep and bind him to his bed before he became aroused. All these preliminaries would have to be attended to before we could go after the treasure itself.

I refused to assent to White's proposition. I explained to him that it was quite cold enough in New York and that the weather must be much more severe in Canada. Besides, I did not fancy sneaking about the cashier's house on creaking snow with the chance of being discovered before I was able to break in. Moreover, there was a likelihood that in dealing with the work we might have to use violence, and I had always kept clear of such "hold up" jobs.

When he saw my reluctance, White proposed taking me to Griffith so that I could satisfy myself by a personal interview. Griffith was then near at hand, but as I did not care to increase my crooked acquaintance I refused the meeting. White was not discouraged by my lack of interest and said he would see me again in the hope that I might change my mind.

On the following day he came to see me again and told me that he had definite information that the bank carried nearly $240,000 in money and securities. That statement made me think more kindly of the robbery and led me to question White more closely.

As a result I learned that Griffith claimed acquaintance with a young man who kept company with a servant girl employed in the cashier's house and that it was through this man that the location of the vault keys had been discovered. That set me to elaborating a new plan for looting the bank which centered around the girl.

At our next meeting I told White that I believed the robbery could be worked in a way different from and more effective than the one which he had outlined, and that if my ideas were carried out I would be willing to go into it. White saw Griffith again and returned to inform me that Griffith would agree to any plan that would give an equally good chance of getting the money.

My scheme was this: the lover of the girl was to induce her to get possession secretly of the chamois-skin bag in which the bank keys were placed and was to give it to her lover for a short time. Griffith was to teach the lover how to take impressions of the keys in wax. The keys should then be returned and the wax impressions brought to me in New York. It would be my part to fashion the false keys from the wax impressions.

Another feature of the scheme was the devising of some means of keeping the clerk away from the bank until 10:30 or 11 o'clock on the night that the robbery was to be effected, so that our work might be done before he returned to go to bed.

White and Griffith were satisfied and went at once to St. Catherine's together. For my part, I gave the matter no more thought, as I was convinced that nothing further would be accomplished. In this I was wrong, however, for in the course of a week or so White returned with the wax impressions, which I found to have been very poorly taken.

I cannot say that I made the keys with any great confidence, and when they were completed, I confess that I felt dubious about their value. Still I decided to go to St. Catherine's with White. I had provided myself with a wig and false whiskers and started at once to look over the field myself.

White knew that I would not take a hand in any such mixed-up proposition as this one appeared to be without first examining carefully into the details.

My first step was to interview Griffith, whom I knew by hearsay to be a weak sort of crook. I visited him at his house, where he lived alone with a woman, and from his answers I learned everything had not been settled as had been represented to me.

For instance, Griffith had never had any direct dealings with the young man who had secured impressions of the keys. In that affair he had relied entirely on a keeper of saloons and gambling rooms. The latter had been the go-between. He had been instructed by White in the art of making wax impressions and had in turn passed on the lesson to the lover. This did not increase my faith in the keys we had.

I determined, however, to talk to the saloon man and was better pleased with result. He explained that he was to meet the bank clerk at 8:30 o'clock that night and would hold him for some two hours. It was then 8 o'clock and I knew we had no time to waste if we were to put the job through.

I was convinced that even if the saloon-keeper was not to be relied on, he could not identify me again on account of my disguise, so I decided we had better make our attempt at once. After he had left us White and I started to the bank.

We had no difficulty in entering by the back door, of which we had the key. It was then only 9 o'clock, but it was so bitterly cold that there were few people about. Our first trouble came when we reached the outside door of the vault. I tried my key, but it did not throw the bolt. Realizing that something was wrong, I went into a closet from which a light could not be seen from the street and spent some time making alterations in the wards of the key with a file.

After trying the key again I succeeded after a time in opening the door. The key of the second door fitted to perfection, as did the key to one of the safes. When we came to the principal safe, however, I saw at once that the key would not work. The lock in question was one of a kind that I had met frequently in my earlier activities and I understood well enough how to overcome it. It was necessary, however, to have seen the original key and not merely a wax impression.

My meaning may be better understood when I explain that the device was in the nature of a combination. The lock contained 8 or 10 tumblers, each of which was lifted to a different height by an equal number of wards in the comb of the key in order to bring the unequally slits in each tumbler on a level so that the "dog" on the bolt could slide into these slits and move the bolt and lock back.

The real secret lay in the fact that the wards of the key were all separate one from the other and held in place by a screw arrangement. The wards could be shifted into different positions. Thus the person locking the safe could disarrange the key wards after the process and had only to rearrange them when he wished to unlock the safe again. In the meantime the altered key would not work in the hands of anyone who got possession of it.

As it happened the impression taken of this key had been a perfectly good one, but instead of making the duplicate key with movable wards I had filed them out of a solid key blank, taking the chance that the cashier might be careless and not change his key wards after locking the safe. As a matter of fact, the cashier had been more careful than I anticipated and had followed the directions of the safe-maker. For that reason the impression we had was absolutely useless.

It is true that we might have taken a large sum of money from the smaller safe, but as we knew that the big safe held the greater treasure it was evident that we would have to leave things undisturbed if we had an idea of trying again.

White was much disappointed and worked at the lock with great persistency despite my protests that he was working himself into a perspiration for nothing. At last he gave up and we held a little conference.

We came to the conclusion that there was nothing further to be done in the bank that night unless we were prepared to force the safe open. This would have taken time and as the clerk might return any moment, we decided to abandon the job for the time being. In the meantime while White was working on the obstreperous key I discovered another serious complication.

When I went to the outer vault door to make sure that I could lock it as I had found it, I was surprised to discover that they key which had unlocked it would not lock it again. This, of course, might prove a hint to the bank people that burglars had been at work and would very likely spoil our chances of a second attempt.

It was now getting near 10 o'clock and after a hasty consultation we saw nothing to do but to take a chance. We figured that if we left the outer vault unlocked it was 100 to 1 in our favor that the cashier would think that he had forgotten to turn the key when he closed the vault. For that reason we closed the door without any further attempt to lock it.

After carefully gathering up everything we had brought with us, we locked the smaller safe and the second vault door and passed out the rear door just in time to avoid the clerk who was returning to the bank. He was not more than a few hundred feet from us but he passed without catching a glimpse of us.

Of course I was thoroughly disgusted with the job and after spending an uncomfortable night on a lounge in Griffith's parlor I promised myself to have no more to do with the affair.

I returned to New York at once, but White was still persistent and kept after me every day begging me not to throw the matter up. At last I consented to go to St. Catherine's again, but I stipulated that White must provide a sleigh and horses to take us to the suspension bridge at Niagara Falls as soon as the loot had been secured.

White agreed and we returned to Canada, determined to blow the safe open with gunpowder. It had been arranged that the saloon-keeper was to lure the clerk away as before and that another man was to be on hand with the required horses and sleigh.

As far as the bank robbery itself was concerned it was simple enough. Everything went without a hitch. We left Griffith's house at 8:30 o'clock in the evening and got into the bank and vault as before. When we came to the big safe I saw that it would not be troublesome. The lock and keyhole were large enough so that we did not have to do any drilling, and very soon I had blown a half-pound of powder into the lock.

While I prepared the fuse, White stayed out in the bank room so that he could watch any movement in the street. Outside it was bitterly cold, the snow was flying in every direction and the wind was howling and driving along in something very like a blizzard. No safer night could have been selected for a safe-blowing.

At a signal from White I applied a match to the fuse and then stepped out closing the vault door behind me. A few seconds later there was a dull roar and when I opened the vault door and allowed the stifling powder smoke to dissipate, I saw that the explosion had sent the safe door open on its hinges.

There before me was stacked a great quantity of money and I noticed that the outer ends of most of the bills had been singed by the heat from the powder. We had already mined the smaller safe and placed the loot in a bag. The second safe held a treasure far greater. Indeed it proved so bulky that it filled up a larger oilcloth bag to the limit of its capacity.

Without lingering any longer we left the bank and set out at once for Griffith's house, where I waited while White went out in search of the promised horses and sleigh. It was then that our troubles began.

After a half hour or so he returned and told me that the saloon-keeper could not find the man who had promised the rig. He hinted that the man had weakened at the last minute and that we would have to find some other means of making our getaway.

In the meantime, the clerk had returned to the bank, and it was not long after that the general hue and cry started. Police officers were rushing here, there and everywhere. We were in a strange town, with no ready method of leaving except by facing the fierce storm with our heavy burdens on our backs.

Luckily Griffith's house was situated on the side of the town towards Niagara, so that we had a good chance of escaping by the side streets. Disagreeable as was the snow, it served as a curtain for our movements and had also the good quality of having covered up our tracks when we left the bank.

There was nothing to do but to rely on the strength of our legs, and we set out at once along the road towards Niagara Falls, where White said there was a tavern or roadhouse where we could hire a team. At that time I was in the heyday of my youth and physical power, but for all that the tramp of a mile and a half through deep snow drifts, carrying a heavy burden, taxed me to the utmost, although it was mere child's play to what was to come.

I ought to explain that White understood horses from A to Z, and that knowledge has often been of great service to the crooks who acted with him in critical jobs. While he went ahead, I had taken my station a little way down the road. The weather was terribly cold, and to gain a little protection I had jumped into a snow drift which covered my body up to my neck.

There behind a corner of rail fence I stood shivering. How I wished myself back in my cozy rooms in New York during that wait of half an hour! At last White returned with a sleigh, and I was never more pleased than when I found myself tucked in under warm buffalo robes.

There was no time to lose and we plunged on through the drifts for all the horses were worth. It was three hours before we reached the old railroad suspension bridge over the Niagara river and once there we drove under a church shed and started at once to investigate.

I was well acquainted with the country on both sides of Niagara Falls as I had often visited there for weeks at a time, and when I saw where we were, I began to expostulate with White. I noticed that he was driving towards the old bridge instead of towards the new bridge which was located some two miles away. I had urged him to take the new bridge because I thought our chances of getting across unmolested would be better, but he told me at once that he knew that the middle section of the roadway over the new structure had not been completed.

White argued that it would be hopeless to try to cross an unfinished bridge in the teeth of a terrific storm, and that the snow would protect us while we climbed the gates at either end of the old bridge and sneaked by the guard houses.

I was by no means as sure as White that we could pass the old bridge. I knew that word of the bank robbery would be telegraphed ahead of us and that every likely way across the river would be carefully guarded. This surmise was soon proven to be true.

Leaving White with the horses I went ahead to reconnoiter, and from the end of the bridge I could see through the windows of the guard house several men. While I stood there I saw two more men come down the road and enter the house. It was then after 3 o'clock in the morning and I soon realized that a strict lookout was being maintained and that there was no chance of our escaping in that direction.

I returned at once to White and reported what I had seen. It was perfectly clear to both of us that our only hope lay in the direction of the new bridge and that we must pass over it no matter what the risk might be.

By that time we had been hours in the driving storm and had suffered enough from cold to take the courage out of the bravest man, but we knew that we must act and act quickly if we did not want to face a long prison sentence. After a hasty snack consisting of a few sandwiches and some tea with brandy in it we set off for the new bridge.

White woke up the stable men in a hotel nearby and left the horses with instructions that they be sent back to the owner the next day. We then made our way to the new bridge and found everything quiet. There was not even a light in the office of the gatehouse. I climbed easily over the gate and unbarred it from the inside so as to admit White. This new bridge was situated about a quarter of a mile below the falls, a flimsy structure which was blown down during a storm some 15 years later.

I have never seen a worse night, nor have I ever encountered a situation more full of danger. Beneath our feet the unfinished flooring of the bridge was covered with a slippery coating of ice formed from the sleet of two days before. The upper layer of snow made the footing only the more treacherous.

Up and down the river the wind was whirling and raging in fierce gusts. The powdery flakes were driven before us in cutting particles, beating into our faces until we were almost blinded. We could hardly breathe in the constant buffeting of the gale. The night was pitch dark and as we edged along we could feel the great bridge structure sway to and from beneath us.

Little by little we made our slow progress out along the bridge for some 150 yards and then while we halted between gusts, we congratulated ourselves that the worst was over. Our joy was only for the moment, however, for as we groped our way a little further our hands found nothing but the empty air and we realized that we were on the very edge of an abyss with the river running by 200 feet below. One false step would have hurled us to death.

We were not long in discovering that we had come to a point where the workmen had stopped work on the roadway and peering through the night we could discern nothing but the nearest crosspieces of steel laid upon a few stringers.

From the edge of this void above which we stood there jutted out a narrow pathway of planks only 12 inches wide laid end to end along the girders, extending an unknown distance into the darkness. Where this slender passage led we could only guess.

As we knelt to examine the nearest plank we found that the snow and sleet had formed in a thick mass of ice, solid and arched to roundness at the top. It would have been difficult to cross under the best of conditions and in the daylight.

We had no idea how far out into the uncertain blackness the thin string of planks extended, nor were we at all certain that once started on the perilous journey we could keep our hold on the slippery surface in the face of the storm. But there was little choice for us. We understood perfectly that we must either make an attempt to cross at the risk of our lives and of our treasure or we must be content to fall into the hands of the Canadian police.

We were not long in choosing the first alternative, although it was like juggling with death. We decided to go forward. It was no pleasant sensation—that vision of the Queen's prison which lay behind and the possibility of an awful fall into the Niagara river which lay before. I am able to this day to recall the feeling of desperate determination which came over me in a moment.

There was one gleam of hope, however, and that was in the fact that the bridge was being constructed as an American enterprise. We figured that it was reasonable to suppose that the floor-laying would have advanced further on the United States side than on the Canadian, and that it was possible that the chasm before us was not as wide as we had first supposed.

Once we had reached our decision to go ahead, we began to plan again. Our first step was to beat our way back to the Canadian shore. There we broke into two stables and foraged about in back yards until we had sufficient quantity of ropes, reins, bits of harness and leather to make a strong cable some 100 feet long.

We first made ourselves strong belts across our waists and shoulders and to these we fastened the cable. The treasure bags were then secured firmly on my back and everything was in readiness for the attempt. George went first, for a wonder, but I guess he did so because he thought I was handicapped by my extra burden.

Then began a feat that still unstrings my nerves even in my old age when I follow it with my mind's eye. We had agreed upon a set of signals on the cable so that each could keep in touch with the other's movements. It was also agreed between us that in case one should lose his grip and fall, and in case the other could not pull him back to safety, under no circumstances should the unfortunate be allowed to hang in midair and freeze to death.

No more words were wasted. White turned to me and grasped my hand, then turned again and began creeping out on the plank. Far below was the roaring river, which we could hear, but not see. The wind swept through the thousand strings of the skeleton bridge, sending forth a weird pandemonium of sounds. The snow was like a thick white curtain, and there was no light. Only a few moments passed and White had been swallowed by the night and snow. I knew he was still alive only by the tugs which came from time to time on the cable.

White's trip I shall describe in his own words as he set them down for me some years afterward. This is his story:

"I had been creeping along inch by inch, and it seemed to me that I must have been on the way an hour before I had covered a score of feet. Then I paused to catch my breath, which had been almost driven out of my body by the fierce shock of the wind. I was compelled to clutch at the planking with all the strength that was in me that I might not be hurled below as far as the cable would permit.

"I resumed the struggle and traversed about a dozen feet more, when a gust struck me and one hand slipped from the plank. Down I went with a crash, and I would probably have plunged to the river had not my right hand come in contact with a girder which happened to be close by.

"With this aid I was able to balance myself until I could regain my place on the plank. These girders later proved considerable aid to me. They were five feet apart and without their help I do not think I would have been able to keep my path.

"I had crawled perhaps 50 feet when I came to the end of the plank and reaching further ahead could feel nothing. Only the girder at my right offered any support. It was about eight inches wide and no doubt extended to the edge of the bridge.

"To my right, however, I thought I saw another plank, but to reach it I had to crawl along the narrow, ice-covered beam. Ahead of me I could make out another girder, but it was far away, and I saw that I may creep to the plank at my right or turn and go back to Shinburn. I decided to make the attempt, but came mighty near slipping from the beam the moment I put my knee on it. The wind seemed to come now with a sort of broadside force. What saved me I do not know, but at last I came to the plank and found a solution to my troubles in part.

"The plank was not so heavy as the others, and had not been so thoroughly frozen to the iron girders. Evidently a strong gust of wind had swept one end of it from its place to the right, thus interrupting my straight passage. I crawled out on this plank, finding it very unsteady owning to the way it rested on the girders. I crept along and bearing to the left came a distance of 15 feet to the resumption of the straight and narrow path which I hoped would lead me to the end of my perilous route.

"In this I was disappointed, for I found one more break in the planking, but this was only a stretch of eight feet, and I traversed it along an ice-covered iron girder. By this time my hands were nearly frozen and my toes had become stiff. If I had dared I would have sat astride the plank and clapped my hands together, but time was precious, and the moments must seem endless to Shinborn.

"I pressed on 10 feet more and found myself on a narrow and terribly slippery piece of planking. In my anxiety to get along I did not discover how dangerous it was until I had taken an insecure hold. Suddenly my hand slipped off and sheering to one side I toppled over.

"Catching the planking with both hands, I hung dangling at arm's length. From time to time I tried to throw my feet up around the plank. For a moment I was bewildered and wasted my efforts trying to get back, and then it occurred to me that by swinging back and forth to get sufficient momentum I could get to the girder that I had just left...

"When I crawled some 10 feet more I came at last to the solid bridge on the American side, and with a feeling of gladness at last scrambled to my feet. Had I dared I would have prayed. By swinging my hands and stamping my feet I soon felt a freer circulation that gave me new life.

"I then signaled back to Shinburn to start, and unloosening the cable I gripped it so as to keep close touch with him in his movements. A tug at the end told me he had started."

That was the story of White's experiences, and my own was not less trying. During the time that White was on his way I held the cable in one hand while I swing the other and stamped my feet to keep warm.

After what seemed a wait of hours I at last received his signal to make the attempt. I felt considerable confidence at the outset, for I argued to myself that what White could do I could do even more easily with my greater physical strength, even though I was weighted down with the heavy bags on my back.

While White was struggling forward, it occurred to me that I could better his method by using a small sectional jimmy which I carried in my pocket. When fitted together it made an implement 18 inches long. This I fastened to a bridle check rein which we had stolen, linking the other end to my belt and leaving about three feet of strap loose.

I began my journey by advancing the point of the tool under the icy covering of the plank where the snow was softer near the wood. I then ripped up a piece of the ice, getting a more secure support for my knee. By repeating this scheme I progressed forward slowly with added confidence.

The work was terribly hard, and my nerves and muscles were strung to the highest tension. By degrees I noticed that my body lost its freezing stiffness, although the skin of my face felt the blasts of snow as if it had been pricked by a myriad of needle points.

After a little I changed my tactics and groped along the side of the planking with my left hand while I advanced my jimmy to pry out chunks of ice for my knees.

At last I came to the place where White had found the shifted board. I was in a quandary for a while, until I considered that if White had found his way I ought to be able to do as well. Looking to the right, I could just make out what appeared to be the end of a joist resting on a girder. I decided to make for it, but when I tried to pry off the ice I found it a solid mass on the surface.

With the burden I carried I felt that I did not dare to crawl on my knees, and instead I sat astraddle on the girder and lying down on my stomach and reaching forward with my gloved hands pulled myself forward inch by inch with a sliding motion.

After a time I reached the plank and resumed my sliding on that. Here I found it more practical to use my jimmy. This I pushed down vertically in the snow crust and used it to drag myself along. When I came to the second break in the planking I employed the same method again, and after that kept on in the same manner until at last I came to the place where White was waiting.

I was not much worse for the adventure, except that as soon as I got on my feet I was seized by a fit of trembling. This was soon cured by a swallow of high-grade brandy. The exhilaration which followed our reunion after our perilous experience with the loot safe may be imagined.

We had still to pass the gate at the further end of the bridge, but although there was a light in the gatehouse, showing there was a watch kept for smugglers, we had little difficulty in sneaking past. It was now 6 o'clock in the morning, and we went at once to a livery stable and hired a team.

We ordered the driver to drive to an inland town 12 miles away. While the team was being hitched I remember that the boss looked curiously at our bags, and I have no doubt that he mistook us for smugglers. After we had gone some distance we made the driver change his course and take us to Tonawanda, half-way between Niagara and Buffalo. On the edge of that town we discharged him, and walking to the other end of the town we hired an old German to drive us into Buffalo, after we had refreshed ourselves with a hot breakfast.

On the road the Niagara Falls train passed us, and no doubt there were officers on it hurrying to Buffalo, which was at that time the headquarters for many border crimes and the place of refuge for a number of crooks. At Buffalo we stopped our carriage a few blocks from the gambling house of a friend of ours, a Boston man, and then walked on to the place, where we left our bags and lay down for a long sleep.

When we awoke we looked over our plunder and counted money and bonds amounting to $240,000. Many of the bills were singed at the edges from the powder explosion, but this did not impair their value. We sorted out the larger bills and placed them in a bag, while the large quantity of smaller bills we left in the care of our friend for safekeeping.

Our first plan was to take a train for Cleveland, to switch off on a local road before we reached that city and then proceed in a southerly direction until we should arrive at a railroad that would take us into Pittsburgh.

While we remained at the gambling house our friend went down to the depot to investigate, and soon returned with the report that three detectives from the central office were on guard there. He also learned that the Canadian officers had arrived in the city even before we had, and that our movements had been traced across the bridge to Niagara to the livery man. The police had even found the old German who drove us into Buffalo and knew precisely the spot where he had left us.

Not daring to take a chance, we remained in hiding that night, and on the following morning I summed up the situation. It was known to the police that we had come to Buffalo either for concealment or to pass through to some other point. There was no extradition under which we could be returned to Canada, as our offence was simple burglary. All the Canadian authorities could hope was to recover some of the loot.

I knew, however, that if the Buffalo police arrested us and got hold of the money very little of it would find its way back to Canada. Besides, White had escaped from jail in Keene, N.H., and there was a reward of $1000 for his recapture. I had escaped from the New Hampshire penitentiary, and there was another $1000 on my head.

Probably the honest public believe that if we had been captured then we would have been returned at once to New Hampshire. The solemn truth of the matter, however, was quite different. Our capture would be sure to expose our identity at once, for a couple of the city detectives knew me.

I have no doubt that our identity would have been kept secret and that the $240,000 would have been split into three parts, of which the smallest would have been returned to the bank, a share given to White and me and as to the other share the less said the better. Thus, if we wanted to keep our loot we must outwit the police.

As we thought it better to get out of Buffalo at all costs, we sent for a young friend of mine who could be trusted and had him hire a carriage. He drove us to Angola in the direction of Cleveland, where we put up at a hotel. While we went to supper we put our bags carelessly under the desk counter, and when we came out I noticed they had been displaced.

Nearby stood two men in earnest conversation, of which White and I were evidently the subject. We smoked our cigars calmly without seeming at all disturbed, and presently one of the men walked up to me and said in an affable manner: "That's a fine team you have in the stable."

"Yes," I answered in a tone that shut off any further conversation.

A few minutes before the train was due and after I had waited until one of the strangers was near enough to hear I stepped up to the desk and handed the clerk the card of a well-known Chicago business house and said: "Give us commercial rates, if you please." As I paid the bill the detective's partner came into the room with a telegram, and the other examined it critically. I had no doubt that we were the subjects of it.

When the train arrived we went aboard and the detectives followed. They had been close at hand and had heard me call for tickets to Cleveland. One of them went into the telegraph office either to wire to Cleveland or to Chicago to find out from the business house I have mentioned whether they had drummers of our description.

By this time the game was getting fast and the trail becoming too hot for comfort. Wherever we turned we heard people discussing the bank robbery at St. Catherine's. Although I wished now we had remained in Buffalo, we played our hand with a bold front. The detectives took a seat in the car with us, but at the opposite end. We had time to think, however, and settled on our plan.

At Cleveland we left the car and walked up to a hackman. Waiting for the sleuths to get near enough to hear, I ordered the driver in a loud voice to take us to the Metropolitan Hotel in a hurry. We were off in short order.

The detectives of course followed us in another carriage, but we were too quick for them. Safe from immediate danger, I bought another bag and transferred the cash to it, leaving nothing in the old bag but a few pieces of soiled linen. White was then driven to the house of a friend on Euclid avenue. We agreed to meet in half an hour near the Cleveland, Pittsburgh, & Rochester railroad depot.

I then went to the Metropolitan Hotel with the old bag in order to throw the hack driver off the trail. It turned out as I had hoped. The detectives had been there and failing to find us started out at once to find the hack driver.

I engaged a room and taking the old bag there I came down again and told the clerk that I would be back directly if anyone called. A few minutes later I had rejoined White and we were walking the railroad ties to the second station beyond the city. There we got a train for Pittsburgh and from there had an uninterrupted journey to New York.

Griffith arrived later from St. Catherine's and stated that his way had been paid by the bank upon his representation that he might be able to find the thieves and arrange for the return of some of the loot. He received one-third of the booty for himself and his Canadian accomplices, but instead of returning to Canada he stayed in New York until every penny he had had been spent, chiefly in playing against faro games. His Canadian friends never got a dollar for their pains.

5 A WAD OF BILLS GETS MARK SHINBORN OUT OF A TIGHT PLACE

Whatever may be the situation at present, in the old days when bank burglary was in its prime there were more ways than one of getting out of legal difficulties, although the evasion of the law was often a pretty costly business. At that time a clever crook had to know a good deal besides the art of safe-cracking—he had to be something of a politician as well. When there were wheels within wheels in the mills of justice, it took no little skill to start proper machinery at the proper time.

The affair I am about to relate was a case in point. I cannot say that I am particularly proud of it from a professional standpoint. It was no credit to George M. White or to me, two criminals of the first class, to be mistaken for a pair of common hold-up men. It was no credit to us that we allowed ourselves to be rounded up by a lot of country policemen and it was certainly nothing in our favor that we were carrying around burglar's tools so carelessly that they could be used against us.

Looking back at it now, the events had a humorous side. We were wanted in a dozen communities for thefts which ran into the hundreds of thousands of dollars, yet one of the most damaging bits of evidence against us was the stealing of a pitcher of ice cream. Both of us had broken jail, there was a large reward out for both, and for that reason it was not pleasant to find ourselves in the lock-up of a small town.

We understood perfectly that brains and money alone would save us and it was the need of unusual action which led to the queer deal in fake warrants and the bribing of a county official. Two cities, neither of which had any valid claim to us, fought for the right of holding White and me only because there was money in it for those who appreciated the underground revenue of crime.

The story begins in the fall of 1866. I had escaped only recently from the state prison in New Hampshire, where I had been sentenced to serve a 10-year term for the robbery of the Walpole Bank in that state. A severe winter followed with very little income for me, and I hung around New York among the crooks to whom I was then well known. Perhaps my closest friend was White, whom I have already mentioned in connection with the St. Catherine's affair.

It may be worthwhile to note that the crook is not greatly different from his more respectable fellow-man. At any rate he takes as much interest in his methods of doing business as does the merchant, for instance, or the head of some going concern. I say this because just then there had appeared an inventor among us who claimed that he had discovered something that would revolutionize burglary.

This supposed genius was John Ryan, who was numbered among my new acquaintances. Ryan came from Buffalo with a set of burglar's tools which he was sure would rip open with the greatest ease almost any vault or safe door in existence. Naturally there were a good many of us who were curious to see Ryan work his wonderful devices.

66

I had not fully recovered from my confinement in prison when a gambler friend of mine asked me to "sneak" the keys of the vault of the county treasurer of Orleans county, New York, at Albion. It was rumored that this official had a great quantity of government bonds in his possession which he was guarding for a friend.

I have always had a dislike for doing house burglary in midwinter. The snow has a peculiar way of creaking under the feet which has more than once aroused sleeping inmates and given not a little trouble. For that reason I refused to act as "sneak," but it occurred to me that here was an excellent opportunity for Ryan to try out his new set of tools.

Accordingly I introduced Ryan to the gambler, and the inventor was only too eager to do the job. Another friend of mine, Palmer, who had been active in engineering my escape in New Hampshire, was willing to take a hand, and in the end I agreed to be one of the party.

We were in difficulties on the money end of the undertaking and so we sought out George White. He was not in need of funds, but he was willing to finance us chiefly because he was curious to get a line on Ryan at work.

A few days later we took the train for Albion, arriving late in the evening in the midst of a snow and wind storm. We entered the treasurer's office at midnight without being molested, and White, Ryan and I tackled the vault door with the new tools. Palmer was the outside man and saved himself much labor.

Like many other inventions, Ryan's was not all we had hoped. For several hours we hammered and cut and gouged at the vault with a stupendous waste of muscular energy. At last we had reduced it to so much junk. It was the queerest safe break I ever saw. The second vault door was of the ordinary flimsy kind and we opened that with our good old-fashioned jimmies.

It may be imagined that poor Ryan had to stand for a lot of comment during the long time we were working. If there was any kind of sarcasm that White and I forgot it was not our fault. Ryan toiled on and on for that one night, but after that the underworld never heard of the remarkable tools again and they were a very sore spot with the inventor ever after.

After we had finished our destruction, all we found was $1100 in 7-30 government bonds, not a very encouraging result. We escaped from the town on a handcar and finally arrived in Buffalo by train. White and I were disgusted and decided that as we were in that part of the state it was foolish to go back to New York empty-handed.

I had in mind the Washington Bank in Corning, and after some argument I induced White to go along with me. I planned to go back to my old methods of "sneaking" into the cashier's house and stealing the safe and vault keys.

We arrived at Corning just after midnight, and at about 2 o'clock in the morning I was prospecting about the cashier's residence when something, I suppose the creaking of our steps in the snow, aroused those within, and a light flared up in one of the rooms.

There was nothing we could do but get away as quickly as possible. It was then that my sweet tooth got the better of my good judgment. Just outside the kitchen door stood a pitcher filled with ice cream, and before we departed I took that and carried it along with me.

After we had eaten the ice cream we went to the railroad depot with the intention of taking the 2 o'clock train for New York. We were sitting comfortably before the stove listening to the whistle of the approaching train, when we were surprised by the entrance of two constables. Some more men followed and locked the door. We were trapped.

White and I did not like the idea of giving up so easily, and in an instant there was a general flashing of revolvers. It was a sharp hand-to-hand tussle while it lasted. One of the constables let fly at me, and I could hear the bullet singing by close to my head. Three men were doing their best to beat me into submission. Thinking the fight had gone about far enough, I jumped on a bench, covered the constable with my gun and asked for a parley. At the same instant the constable raised his weapon and fired. It would have been all over for me had not the trigger clicked harmlessly. It was a close call.

In the meantime White had fared badly in the hands of several others. I could see from where I stood that the blood was running freely from several cuts on his head and face. His assailants were pounding him systematically and with telling effect.

Still standing on the bench, I edged into a corner and threatened to shoot the first man who made a hostile movement. That quieted things down, and we saw that our only chance was to surrender in the face of odds.

By that time since all hands were willing to talk, I learned that we were supposed to be desperate hold-up men. It seems a storekeeper at Addison, eight miles away, had been attacked the day before, beaten into insensibility, and robbed of a large sum of money and the constables were convinced that we were the criminals. There was no use to argue that we were not, so we were marched off to the lock-up. Our valises containing burglar's tools were found at the station and that was another point against us.

On the other hand we pointed out that we had come down on the train from Buffalo and were the only passengers who got off at Corning. This proved to be something in our favor, for the conductor of the train afterwards corroborated our statement.

In the afternoon we were whisked off to Addison and there were confronted with the storekeeper. He said positively that I was not one of the two men who had held him up but was not so sure in the case of White. The matter began to look better for us when somebody remembered the ice cream pitcher. It was learned that it had been taken from the house of the bank cashier, so that the authorities were satisfied that if we were not hold-up men, we were criminals of some sort.

When we saw that our other stories did not prove convincing enough to gain our freedom, White let it be known that we were special envoys of the New York police sent out by Capt. Jordan of the New York department to hunt up certain desperate crooks who were thought to be operating in the neighborhood.

In the meantime we had been bound over for the action of the grand jury and were kept in a hotel in Corning under guard. This was done because it was believed that we could obtain bail and that we might be what we pretended we were, special men from the New York department.

Capt. Jordan delayed his answer to inquiries and for several days we remained at the hotel enjoying the best of treatment. We had become local celebrities, for the fracas with the constables had been magnified by the county newspapers into a shooting affair with all the dime novel scenery in which we figured as bandits.

That sort of publicity did not help us inasmuch as it turned the

70

attention of the police all over the state towards us. It was only a day or two after our arrest when Bob Watts, a Buffalo detective, appeared on the scene. Watts knew me perfectly well and I knew him, but he did not pretend that he had ever seen me before and of course I was not eager to announce my identity. I saw his game at once, however, and knew he was after the reward offered for me in the state of New Hampshire. I understood that he would not let anyone else in on that business if he could help it.

It is curious how old crimes will crop up as soon as a crook gets into trouble. Here was a notable instance. It was nine years since Watts and I had come together before, but his memory of the old case was enough to make it bad for me.

That old offense was one of my early breaks from jail, and, with the exception of Watts, there was nobody who could have made me trouble on that score. The incident is clear in my memory, although I gained nothing by it.

It was in the late fifties, and I had crossed over from Canada intending to go to Rochester. As I passed through Albion, however, I saw that Dan Rice's circus was going to show there, so I left my train for a day's amusement. On the following day I met a pair of pretty young country girls and took them to the circus with me.

In walking about the town I spotted a large safe in the general store and decided to look at it. I found out where the storekeeper lived and, after making my farewell bow to the girls, I gave up my hotel room; but instead of taking the next train I hid in a clump of woods until night and then went to the storekeeper's house.

I had no difficulty in entering the house. I found the merchant asleep, took his trousers, and carried them outside. The keys for the safe were in his pocket. There was also one solitary French five-franc piece, which I took.

Without waiting any longer, I went down to the store, for which I had no key. Not wishing to force the door, which was well-fastened, I mounted on a ladder to the second story window in the rear of the store. Here I met with a new difficulty, for when I flashed a match against the glass I saw a man sleeping in a bed.

As I could not hope to do the job that night, I took wax impressions of the keys and went back to the storekeeper's house again. I realized that I must return his keys to his pocket from which I had taken them, so that he would have no suspicion of the robbery I was planning.

I broke in again and was just putting the trousers back on the chair when the man's wife woke up and screamed. I beat a hasty retreat and got away, but was arrested in Rochester two days later, and the finding of the five-franc piece in my possession clinched the case against me.

Besides this the police found an express office receipt which showed I had sent a package to Buffalo. I was taken back to Albion and given a hearing, at which the storekeeper swore to his five-franc piece, making his evidence doubly sure by naming the date of its issue.

It was then that I first saw Bob Watts. He came on from Buffalo with the express package I had sent, and from it produced some fine wax impressions of the keys to the storekeeper's safe. The police had me "dead to rights" and I saw that my only hope was to break jail.

I soon discovered a way that I thought might be successful if I could get my friends busy, but I would have to wait a month until I could get a canal-boat man who was my fellow prisoner to take a note to them. His sentence expired at that time.

That seemed too long and I set to work on another scheme. After I had been confined for two weeks a young girl was brought in an placed in the debtor's room upstairs. I noticed that whenever her meals were brought in a heavy iron door from the kitchen of the sheriff's house was opened and then a second door which led to the cell corridor. The second door had a hole about five feet from the floor through which the food was passed to the prisoners.

There was, however, no way of getting food to the debtor's room except by direct delivery, so that when the turnkey brought meals to the girl he had to enter the cell hall and go upstairs, leaving the kitchen girl to lock the door behind him.

I figured that someday the kitchen girl would be careless and leave the key in the ,lock and that she would not take the trouble to close the heavy outer door. One day when the sheriff and his family were away precisely what I hoped for happened. The turnkey came in with food for the girl prisoner and the kitchen maid left the key in the lock.

All I had to do was put my arm through the food hole, turn the key, shut the door again, relock it and take the key. The outer door I found open as I had expected. I passed out through the kitchen, smiling politely at the kitchen girl, and made for the nearest woods. That was the last seen of me in that neighborhood for many years.

That was the incident that made me known to Bob Watts and he remembered me at once. He knew I was Mark Shinborn and knew there was $1000 waiting for him as soon as he got me over into New Hampshire. All he needed was sufficient authority to take me out of jail.

After he had made sure of my identity, he hurried back to Buffalo and there he swore out a "fake" warrant charging White and me with burglary in that city. In the meantime we had been shifted to the county jail in Bath and in a few days Watts was back to that town. He displayed his warrant and demanded that the sheriff turn us over at once.

We were not dupes to the activities of Watts and understood very well that unless we could outwit him New Hampshire would be our destination. We talked of breaking jail, but as the place was full of stool pigeons we soon saw that the attempt was practically hopeless.

White and I debated the question at length and finally came to the conclusion that if Watts could get a fake warrant in Buffalo, we could get one in New York. Acting upon this idea, we sent a message to our friends in the latter city to instruct them to obtain the necessary document and also to bring us "the sinews of war."

As soon as the cash arrived we retained a lawyer and told him to spare no expense in our defense. In the meantime circumstances had developed which seemed to prove that the supposed hold-up of the merchant for which we were held was a fraud and designed to defraud the man's creditors. Under ordinary circumstances that ought to have been enough to secure our freedom.

The warrant held by Watts was our chief stumbling block, and as the last day of the sitting of the grand jury approached we began to worry about the result. In the nick of time, however, a New York man, chief clerk of a city judge of New York, arrived with a warrant for our arrest, charging us with everything short of murder.

He served the warrant on a county official and maintained that it must take precedence over the Addison warrant and every other claim, including that of Watts.

"I must have these men," he insisted to the official. "I must take them back to New York. We know them to be a desperate pair of rascals and New York wants them and must have them. We can put them away for a certainty, while you fellows may not even have a case against them here or in Buffalo. If they go at large the blame will be on your head."

It was now flatly up to the official to determine which warrant he would honor. I was in doubt as to the outcome, but our lawyer said the sheriff would recognize the New York one as a special favor to him.

We were waiting for the report of the grand jury one afternoon around 1 o'clock when the official called us aside. "I have no further claim," he said, "but there are two warrants for you boys, one from Buffalo and one from New York."

I asked him which one he would recognize, and after shifting about a bit he replied: "Detective Watts was the first in the field and I suppose I must give him the preference. He's in town now and has asked me to turn you fellows over to him so he can get away on the evening train."

"Why, how is this," said I, "Our lawyer assured us you would favor him and give the New York warrant the preference."

At that he pretended to get mighty mad and blurted out: "Let me tell you I'm running things in this county and not your lawyer."

It was plain to me what he was after and that there had been some sort of cash offer from somebody interested, otherwise he would not have ignored our lawyer's request. We realized that prompt action was needed if we did not expect to be swamped with trumps on this last deal.

"Mr. Blank," I said, taking the bull by the horns, "you told our lawyer that you would turn us over to the New York officer, who really has a right to us. We believe, too, that we can get real justice there, while from Buffalo we'll get none. You know we are innocent of this Addison affair. Now, we would like to come to some agreement with you, and perhaps we can make it an object to you to turn us over to the New York police. If you will withdraw for a minute we will consult together on this matter."

While I was making this little speech I watched the official closely for any indication of wounded dignity but saw none. On the contrary I was convinced that my first impression was correct and that the only question was how much we would give.

Without any more talk he stepped out into the next room, leaving the door open. George and I consulted in whispers. I told White that the deal was up to him. White was furnishing the money and I insisted that he would carry through the negotiations. I told him that I was sure that the official would back and fill if the bribe was offered under more than two pairs of eyes. I suggested that he and the other man get together while I stepped out into the hallway between our room and the iron door which led to the cell corridor.

After we had argued it out, I called the other negotiator and left him to talk the matter over with White. I then stepped out into the corridor. White did not keep him waiting long, and without speaking he put his hand in his pocket and drew out a fat roll of greenbacks.

"That's the kind of stuff," he said. "Let's get down to hard pan. What's the price? What's it worth? Bob Watts isn't a fleabite to me."

The official fidgeted about for a while, but soon began a long explanation of the risks he was taking and how well he ought to be paid. After some talk back and forth, he came out flat-footed for $1000.

Then George called me in and we sent for our attorney. The lawyer, when he learned the particulars, said we were wasting our money and said there was no need of turning over the sum as he would fix the matter himself. George, however, was in no humor for taking chances and declared he would pay the bribe anyway.

As for me, I would have felt satisfied if the official or anybody else had received $10,000, provided I was not turned over to Watts, although I am still of the opinion that White and I played in a game against stacked cards.

About 3 o'clock the official summoned us to the office of the jail in charge of the turnkey. Our lawyer was on hand, and from the appearance of things I feared that there had been another hitch in the negotiations. I hoped that our man had not reconsidered his decision. We did not long remain in suspense.

"Detective Watts is on the rampage," began the official, "and says he is bound to get you fellows, if he has to use force. He evidently means what he says, for he has got two more officers with him, and he swears that by hook or by crook he will take you back to Buffalo tonight."

He seemed to enjoy our look of disappointment, but it proved that he was only trying us out.

"If I turn you over to the New York officers here," he continued,

"Watts may attempt to take you away at the depot on the plea that his warrant antedates the one from New York. For that reason I am going to have you men ironed hand and foot and am going to take you as far as Corning, where I shall turn you over to the New York men."

This speech reassured us completely. "You could not have thought of anything better," said I, smiling and shaking his hand. Then we got down to a business that was more pleasant to him than our praises—the payment to him of the money we had agreed upon. It was our strongest argument and more potent than any plea for justice.

White paid the lawyer the remainder of his fee and then by a quick turn of his hand passed into the hand of the official $1000 in bills. It disappeared in a second. Orders were issued at once that our irons be brought in and the manacles were placed on our hands and feet. For once we were glad to wear them and looking like a pair of dangerous bandits, we were marched through the town, followed by a crowd of men and boys.

The citizens must have thought the authorities believed us to be a desperate couple, for the official and two deputies clung to us like unpaid gas bills. Detective Watts with his reinforcements and a big crowd were at the station before us, but the promised clash did not occur.

To be sure, Watts looked as if he could bite a tenpenny nail and when White and I smiled at him in triumph he repaid us with a glare of disappointment. We got on the train with the sheriff and one deputy, while Watts and his men followed in the same car. Once at Corning where we were to change cars, our captors invited us to a substantial meal with plenty of wine. It was a merry dinner, all the more so because as we were eating the Buffalo train pulled in and pulled out again taking with it the disconsolate Watts and his followers. He had realized at last that although he held the right bower there is sometimes a joker in the pack.

A little later the New York train came along and the sheriff handed us over to the New York officer and we were off. The handcuffs were still on our wrists and the shackles on our ankles and as we clanked into the passenger coach we were the object of no little attention.

White and I enjoyed the situation, but the irons were not to our liking. Accordingly, we asked our guardian to remove them, but he advised us to leave them on for a little longer. Half an hour later he proceeded to take them off to the great surprise of our fellow passengers who were convinced that we were murderers at the very least. The irons were left at Elmira to be sent back to the sheriff.

We reached New York in the best of spirits and were arraigned at once before a city judge in his private office. A New York lawyer who represented us stated that the warrant upon which we were arrested had really no basis for issue and that the whole affair had grown out of an ordinary family quarrel. We were released on a nominal bail and never heard more from the case.

6 HOW SHINBORN CLEANED UP $20,000 AT SPRINGFIELD

I can't tell where the idea originated, but it has come to be a pretty general impression that crooks, especially those of the more daring sort, are always great hulking fellows, burly—that's the word—burly six-footers and giants in physical strength. Whenever I read of one of these huge ruffians of the Bill Sikes type I smile to myself and think of "Little Dick" Moore, as plucky and skillful a bantam burglar as ever blew a safe or handled a jimmy.

Dick stood a very few inches over five feet in height and weighed about 125 pounds, yet what he lacked in size he more than made up in courage and resourcefulness. I have known criminals of many kinds, but I recall few that I would rather have at my side in a tight place than this same "Little Dick." Besides, I had a professional admiration for him because once on a job he carried it through in a workmanlike manner that I was bound to respect.

On several occasions Dick asked me to help him out in his individual jobs, and as I had a strong liking for the man in spite of his peculiarities I usually went along with him. Strange to say, although we were successful when working alone, when we were together we seldom got away with any very large amount of loot. Dick was an unusually capable burglar, but he had no mind for details, and most of his failures occurred because he did not take the necessary precautions beforehand.

For all that, I liked to work with Dick and more than once made a tidy little haul with him. I remember one incident particularly well because the pair of us took $20,000 from under the very noses of a gang of safe-breakers and turned the trick without much difficulty while they were thinking things over. The affair may be recalled by some of the older residents of the state, for it occurred in Springfield in 1868.

For some time before we made our break George White, whom I have mentioned in other articles, and four other men, "Eddie" Hughes, "Gus" Fisher, "Johnny" Ryan and "Little Dick" had been prospecting about the offices of one of the railroads in Springfield with an idea of looting the safe on the day before pay day.

They knew that the payroll ran up into the thousands and that the men got their money every two weeks. I don't know what was the matter with White, who was usually prompt enough when there was any cash to be had, but he brought his crowd to Springfield twice and then took them away again without accomplishing anything.

It was after the second trip that "Little Dick" became disgusted and sought me out with the proposition that we would put the deal through before White got busy again. Dick had all the information we needed, and besides he was so good a worker that I decided the thing was worth a trial.

He told me the following Saturday was pay day and that as the money was placed in the safe on Friday night, that would be our best time. I agreed to go along, and, after hearing some further details, decided that our quickest method would be to blow the safe.

Accordingly on Friday night we arrived in Springfield, bringing with us the necessary tools and a supply of powder. The building was not an easy one to tackle, and that doubtless was one of the reasons which deterred White and his crowd. It stood on one side of the switching yard some 400 yards from the depot, with its back to the network of tracks and its front facing on a narrow street.

Dick had already found out where a ladder was to be had, and at about 11 o'clock at night we crept along the tracks to the rear of the place. Engines and cars were plying back and forth along the rails, but they were rather a help than a hindrance to us, and the clatter they made deadened any sound of our operations.

I climbed up on the yard side to the second floor, jimmied the window and got into the office with little trouble. "Little Dick" followed, drawing the ladder up after him. We then closed the window and set to work to the accompaniment of the clanking and chugging of the passing trains.

Our first problem was to open the vault, but there we were fortunate, for we found the keys in a little bag in one of the office desks. The vault keys were plain affairs and worked readily, but the key to the safe was one of those combination makes which had caused me so much bother at St. Catherine's. I knew I could manage it well enough if I had time to rearrange the wards, but that would have meant a couple of hours of studying. I determined to take a chance and blow the lock instead.

That was simple, as the safe had a large keyhole in which I placed the powder and then attached the fuse. When all was in readiness, we waited for 15 minutes until we heard a heavy passenger train rumbling in toward the depot and just as it passed we touched off the powder and shut the vault door. The sound of the explosion was effectually deadened by the noise of the train.

When the smoke had cleared away, we looked into the safe and saw it heaped full with little envelopes, each containing the wages of some employee of the company. Without waiting to open them we stuffed them into a bag, closed the vault door and left the office by the front without bothering to remove the ladder.

We caught an early morning train back to New York and when we were safe in that city counted over our spoils. We were $20,000 richer for our night's work. Of course, the newspapers made the usual row over the robbery and when White read the story I can imagine his feelings. When I met him a little later he only laughed and shook his head knowingly. I saw he suspected me, but I never acknowledged the job even to him.

As to "Little Dick," nobody ever suspected him of that theft or a score of others in which he had a hand. I have never known a clever criminal— and Dick was certainly clever—who attracted so little attention from the police. For years he was associated with crooks of the first class and was the equal of any of them in many respects, but he remained less known than any other man of like skill with whom I have been acquainted.

Of course, his size was in his favor; he looked like anything but a desperate character, but I do not think the smallness of his stature had as much to do with keeping him clear of the law as the bigness of his head. He was very wise, was Dick.

In nearly every robbery in which he was engaged Dick was content to let some other crook more familiar with the police take the lead. In those days it was the custom to pay over the proper percentage on the gross loot to the right officials and that duty always fell to the man who was the head of the gang. Dick had no liking for that sort of negotiating and usually managed to remain peacefully insignificant.

If ever I shall write a book about the criminals I have known, I would be sure to do full justice to Dick Moore. He was a burglar of extraordinary ability. He was one of a very few men who ever made a success in a line which was peculiarly my own—I mean the art of "sneaking."

No man who hasn't tried it can realize fully how formidable an undertaking it is to enter a darkened house in the middle of the night. Anything may happen, and the least mistake may bring imprisonment or worse. It is one thing to pick a lock and raise a window, to go through the lower rooms of a house and get away with the silver or whatever is portable. It is quite another thing to prowl about bedrooms where people are asleep.

Now in the old days of key safes a good sneak was in great demand, and good sneaks were few and far between. Bungling workers jimmied windows, hacked and blew safes and were forever getting into trouble from the commotion they stirred up.

The method of a really capable safe burglar was entirely different. What he wanted was the keys of the building he was to rob and the keys of the vault and safes inside the building. That was where the "sneak" came in. It was his duty to effect an entrance in the house of the banker or merchant whose store or bank was to be visited. Once inside, the sneak crept up into the bedroom, tiptoed to the chair near the bed, fumbled in trousers' pockets and found the keys he wanted.

Then he took the keys to a more convenient place, made wax impressions of them and when that had been done returned them to the pockets where he had found them, locked up the house again and left without disturbing anything. The prospective victim awoke in the morning without suspecting that he had been visited, and the burglars, with the key impression in their possession, could wait until a convenient time to do their work.

Both Dick and I had trained ourselves for a number of years in the best methods of sneaking. I know that I could rummage about a house almost without relying on my eyes. My hearing became sharpened so that I could detect the slightest sound and I grew to have a sort of sixth sense of feeling. I had an instinct for avoiding obstacles and could navigate around unfamiliar rooms without knocking against tables or chairs. I never carried a flash lantern and seldom used a match.

That is what it means to be a good sneak, and "Little Dick" was one of the best. Besides he was a safe burglar of no small reputation among his fellow crooks. He was a shrewd bit of a man, but had one weakness that was understood by all his friends. He was known everywhere in the underworld as an inveterate liar and his name was seldom mentioned without some stupendous tale to match it.

In those days the aristocrats of crime, of whom Dick was one, were always welcome to the largest and best rooms in the saloons and gambling houses which they frequented. There they foregathered to spend their money and discuss their adventures. There were many wild stories told, but Dick always managed to relate circumstances that put all the rest in the shade.

His story of the toughest man he had ever known became a classic among his associates. They delighted to get him started with tales of reptiles, heaping on the horrors. Dick would sit quiet for a while and then break in with a remark that all that had gone before was nothing.

"I was acquainted with a man who was so tough," he would say with an air of deep conviction, "that he had no fear of the worst kind of rattlesnake. Why, once I saw him bitten by one of the most poisonous kind, but he just laughed at the accident and when he looked a minute later there was the snake lying stiff and dead. The man wasn't troubled at all."

Dick was the most positive individual I have ever met. You could not argue with him once he had made up his mind. I have always said that he bore the same relation to the human family that a crabapple tree bears to the rest of the fruit trees in an orchard. For all that Dick was a good friend of mine and I had impressed him so thoroughly that he was shy about lying to me.

I had a rather unusual adventure with him in a little town some 12 miles from Syracuse, N.Y., in the late sixties. I was idling about New York between jobs when Dick came to me with the wax impressions of a comb key to a Herring safe. He said it was a duplicate of a key to a safe in a combined bank and general store in the town in question and that there was a considerable sum of money to be had.

Dick had sneaked into the cashier's house and made his impressions without being detected. He had also watched the bank and found that when the cashier opened the safe the key of the small strongbox was still in the lock. This circumstance explained to him why he had not found the strongbox key in the cashier's trousers and he was cocksure that the strongbox key always remained in the lock because the handle was bent, as he put it, by being knocked by the outer door of the safe.

Dick told me that one of the clerks slept in the store at night with a sword, a musket, and a bayonet close by him. On Sunday evening, however, the clerk took an hour or two off to visit his home and did not return until 10 o'clock.

On that account we decided to make our attempt on Sunday evening, and with that in view we hired a rig in Syracuse and drove over to the town at nightfall. Although it was early, it was quite dark, and after we had put up our horse in a church shed we went on to watch the bank. We had not been long on the lookout when Dick came back to me and reported that there was a dog on the premises.

We concluded that the clerk would probably take the animal with him when he went out, and if he did not we thought we would have a try at the place anyway. We kept a sharp eye on the bank until about 8 o'clock, and then we saw the clerk come out, but without the dog. That seemed unfortunate, for it seemed certain that if the dog began to bark we were pretty sure to have a run-in with the citizens, and we were not looking for that kind of fracas.

It was a forbidding-looking job when we came to examine it close at hand. The building was well secured with heavy front doors and solid wooden shutters on all the windows except the front show window. To jimmy the door at that early hour was out of the question, so I determined to force the shutters on a window on a side street. Before doing this, however, I took the precaution of rattling the front door, and when I did so the dog set up a noisy howling. As there was a light, I could see him easily, a large black and tan, young and overgrown.

Both Dick and I saw that there was no use taking a chance and came to the conclusion that we had better let the matter rest until we could devise some scheme for getting rid of the dog. We drove back to Syracuse and remained there until the following evening.

Then we drove over again, fully determined to kidnap the four-footed watchman. On this night the store was kept open until 9:30 o'clock, and it was our idea to steal the dog at once in the belief that as soon as he was missing the clerk would scour the town for his pet. In the meantime we would enter the store, open the safe in the banking office, steal the contents and get away before the clerk came back.

We planted ourselves under a tree near the store and waited. At last, when it was about 9 o'clock, several people left the place and with them came the dog. He ran sniffing about as young dogs will and when he came to the side of the store where we stood I tempted him with a bit of ox-liver. At first he was shy, but after a little I made friends with him.

I had provided myself with a leash, hoping to lead him away, but he pulled back and would not be persuaded. Then Dick took a hand. He brought a leather muzzle from Syracuse which was designed to fit the dog up to the neck and to leave only the nostrils free. It was tight enough to jam the animal's jaws together.

There was a lively tussle while it lasted, but the wiry little man finally got a grip on his squirming antagonist, forced the muzzle in place, and the pair of us managed to get the dog over a fence to a neighboring lawn where we tied his legs so that he was absolutely helpless.

Dick was not in the best of humor after what he considered so much useless labor. He had wished at the outset either to poison the beast or to catch and kill him on the spot, but I have always had a warm spot for dumb animals and refused to listen to any plan that would deprive the poor dog of his life.

I carried him off in my arms to a place where we had left our wagon and laid him on the grass after securing him to a tree by the leash. We then resumed our guard of the bank. At 9:30 the proprietor and one clerk left the place and a little later we saw the second clerk, who slept in the store, come to the door and begin whistling for the dog.

When he got no response he went back into the store, put out all the lights but one and then came out on the street again. He walked away whistling and calling. In a minute I was at the store door and had jimmied it open. While Dick remained outside to give me the "office" in case anybody came past, so that I might hide, I entered the place and made my way to the bank rooms. These were located at the corner of the building at the intersection of two streets.

I went at once to the safe and had no difficulty in opening it with the false key we had made. I then reached for the strongbox expecting to find the key in the lock, as Dick had told me it was sure to be, but to my consternation no key was there.

I searched all the little drawers in the safe, jimmied all the doors under the bank room counter but saw no trace of any key. Meanwhile the clerk was likely to return at any minute and I scurried about like mad trying to discover some way of forcing open the strongbox. That would have been easy if I had brought along the proper tools, but all I had with me was my 22-inch sectional jimmy. Even that would have been suitable if I had a four-pound hammer. But where was I to get the hammer?

I did anything but bless Dick for his cocksureness about the strongbox key. With the clerk expected momentarily we had no time to break into a blacksmith shop to steal a hammer, and my only hope was that I might fine one on the premises or at least come at an axe.

I hustled all over the shop, burning match after match in my quest, but found nothing that would help me. I was about to give up in disgust when

Dick opened the front door and called to me: "He's coming back. I hear his whistle."

Without more ado I shoved the box back into the safe and hurriedly locked the door. I then joined Dick. It was just in the nick of time, for the clerk was already near the bank, whistling as he came. He had been absent for about 30 minutes.

We hurried at once to the place where we had left the dog. I cut the cords that bound his feet, removed the muzzle and leash, and then offered him some ox-liver as a reward. He was in no mood for our company, however, and the instant he was free he set off howling and crying and never stopped until he reached his master.

We drove off towards Syracuse as crestfallen a pair of burglars as can be imagined. But that was not the end of our misfortunes, for in speeding through the dark across a bridge which spanned the Erie canal, the right wheels of our buggy ran up on one of the arched iron stringers that support the roadway and dumped us over. Luckily the horse did not bolt—he was evidently used to that kind of accident—and we soon extricated ourselves from beneath the rig not much worse for the toss.

I was anything but pleased with the whole attempt, and as it was now close to midnight I hurried away from Dick to catch the 12 o'clock train for New York, and succeeded by a pretty narrow margin. Dick patched up the buggy as best he could and drove it to the livery stable where we had hired it and left it standing outside the door. He got back to New York in due time.

Six months passed and in all that time Dick was still think about how he could beat that bank. He came to me again and suggested that I go after the place with him. This I refused absolutely to do. I knew that clerk was still sleeping in the premises, and I saw at once that any plan that Dick could make would involve violence. I had no intention of going into hold-up work, which was never in my line.

Dick's scheme was to wait for a bad night, enter the place just after the proprietor left and to surprise the clerk before he had a chance to get his sword or gun. I had kept Dick's key since our last attempt and had entrusted it to the hands of a "square" friend of mine, who took care of many things for me that I did not dare keep in my own rooms.

When Dick saw that I would not go with him he demanded the key. I told him it was safely planted and whenever he was ready to make the try I would get it for him. I suggested that he go to the cashier's house again for the purpose of sneaking the strongbox key, but he said that would not be necessary, as the strongbox could be easily forced with the aid of a hammer and chisel.

Some days later he came to me again and told me that he had arranged with two other men to put through his hold-up. He wanted the safe key at once, but I told him that before I gave it to him he would have to agree to give me my "bit" out of the robbery. I argued that if it had not been for his lack of judgment we would have done the job properly the first time we tried it.

He accepted my proposition without much argument and I got the key for him. I knew the men he had selected by reputation well enough to understand that if there was any rough work to be done there would be no dilly-dallying so far as they were concerned. My judgment was justified by what followed.

Dick and his two pals arrived in the town early one weekday evening and planted themselves outside the store so that they could keep tabs on everything that happened. At about 9:30 o'clock the proprietor left the place, followed by one of his clerks. The other clerk remained as usual, with his dog, his sword, his musket and a new revolver which had been added to the arsenal since Dick and I visited the place before.

Unfortunately for himself, the clerk did not lock the door immediately after the departure of his employer, but set to work to put out the lights all over the building. Dick and his two pals crept out from their place of concealment as soon as they were sure there was nobody within earshot and walked silently into the place.

The clerk turned quickly and found himself face to face with a masked man armed with a revolver. Despite his fright, however, he was game enough and regardless of his peril gave a bound over the counter towards the niche where his weapons were kept.

The other burglars had been too quick for him, and as he ran toward that end of the room he was confronted by two more masked men who had slipped by him unnoticed. It was an easy manner for Moore and his companions to overpower the man who in the shock of the moment forgot even to yell for help.

To me one of the most curious things about the whole adventure was the behavior of the dog. When we had tackled him first he was full of fight and would bark as lustily as any animal of his size I have ever seen. On this occasion, however, Dick told me that the beast dodged off into the rear of the store and slunk under one of the farthest counters with no more noise than a few plaintive whimpers. I have always thought that the fright Dick and I gave him on our previous visit must have taken all the courage out of him. That was a lucky thing for the burglars.

They had come prepared to make a fight if necessary and were convinced that the clerk would shout and that the dog would howl before they had a chance to gag the one and shoot the other. They fully expected that the disturbance would arouse the neighbors, but they figured that by forcing the strongbox in a hurry they could get away before the citizens arrived in force and that at the worst they would only be a little shooting.

As it happened nothing of the sort occurred. Nobody passed the bank during the struggle with the clerk, and the hubbub had gone quite unnoticed. In view of the fact Dick and his aides went to work more deliberately than they had intended.

After they had gagged the clerk they bound him to his couch, and then one of the men was placed on the outside as a lookout. As Dick was the skilled workman of the trio he was given the duty of opening the safe and the strongbox. He planned to leave things in such shape that the burglary would not be discovered until the morning, thus giving the gang plenty of time to make a good getaway.

They knew that if a "tumble" should come before they escaped the news of the break would be telegraphed to Syracuse and the police would plant themselves on all inleading roads and would be supplied with information as to the rig the burglars had. That last item, by the way, was always a good clue, for any knowing police department in those days would find out at once what strangers had hired teams during the previous night.

It was arranged that the outside man was to signal by a series of knocks on the window as soon as anyone approached, and the burglars were then to close the safe door at once and conceal themselves under the bank counter. There was only one such interruption and the signal worked so well that the passerby went on his way without the slightest suspicion.

The safe offered no trouble, for the key worked as well as it had done before. The box inside proved equally easy and was opened with a half-dozen well directed blows on the head of a chisel with an eight-pound sledge hammer. Moore found what appeared to be a fine amount of loot and tucked it away hastily in a bag. He then replaced the strongbox and shut and locked the safe door.

As the job had been done in a skilled way without so much as the jimmying of a door or window, the only thing that could lead to early detection was any outcry the clerk might make. He was securely bound and gagged, but fearing that he might work out of his bonds, the burglars took a few additional precautions before they left.

While one man stood guard with his revolver, the other untied the clerk, removed the gag and gave him a drink of water. He was then tied up again in a more comfortable position on his couch and the gag was replaced.

His bed was in a position not far from the counter and to make his silence doubly sure, Moore and his associates rigged up a device which was ingenious to say the least. They took the clerk's own musket, placed it on the counter so that it pointed directly at him and then fastened one end of a cord to the gun and the other to the clerk's arm.

When all these arrangements were completed Moore warned the clerk that the least move might mean instant death and that his only safety lay in remaining still until somebody released him in the morning. It is certain that the victim of this scheme must have put in about as uncomfortable a night as anyone could experience, but his disgust must have been great in the morning when he discovered that the musket was not cocked and that the cord was not tied to the trigger.

Without delaying any longer the trio left the bank, and after scouting about to see that all was quiet, went back to their rig and drove off to Syracuse. There they returned the horse and wagon to the livery stable and took the first train for Schenectady, where they stopped at the hotel of a friend long enough to divide the money, which amounted to a little over $28,000.

"Little Dick" told his pals that he would have to have $6500 out of the spoils for my share, as that was the amount agreed upon, but the other two men could not see that proposition, and sent him to me with $2500. I was by no means willing to take so small a share and set to work to play a little politics to get what belonged to me.

As it happened, Dick had been given the required 10 per cent of the gross amount which was to be passed over to pay for protection in New York. He was to meet the man who was to act as collector that night, and intended to make the payment. When I found this out I hunted up the collector before Dick could reach him and put the case up to him so strongly that he agreed to refuse the 10 per cent dividend until I was satisfied.

Accordingly when Moore saw our friend that night he was met with a refusal. The collector said that he would have nothing to do with the money because it had "blood on it," that is to say that it was secured by violence. Dick came to me again as I had expected and I told him that he had better see his pals in a hurry and tell them that unless they let me straighten out their difficulties they were in a fair way of getting into trouble with the police.

This argument had a good effect on Dick's associates, and it was not long before I received my proper share of $6500, although I had not anything to do with the actual robbery.

7 TRUE STORY OF THE GREAT SOUTH NORWALK BANK ROBBERY

I have sat into some stiff games in my time and have seen great sums lost and won over the gaming tables in this country and abroad, but my oddest experience in the realm of chance was that which gained me $100,000 during a session at poker in which I did not hold a card. In fact, I did not play at all.

This is not one of the thousand and one tales of freak hands which are told of the national pastime. Like most of my stories it has to do with a bank robbery—the looting of the South Norwalk, Ct. National Bank. Poker, however, had an important part in it and it was poker that came near costing George White, "Little Dick" Moore, Shell Hamilton and me a fine bit of plunder and our freedom as well.

I know just how exciting it is when fortune flirts pleasantly with a player or fades away at the tail of a draw. That is a situation that calls for a goodly amount of nerve. Here is one that, to my mind, beats it fifty ways.

Imagine, if you will, a safe-breaker touching off a fuse in a bank vault while a group of worthy citizens are dallying with the cards only a few yards away. Imagine the game interrupted by a heavy explosion and the crash of breaking glass. Imagine the players rushing out into the street to see what had happened. Imagine the burglar hesitating between flight empty-handed and quick action that would bring him a huge amount of swag and bonds. Just think for a minute of the excitement of those seconds while he waited to find out which way his luck would turn.

All that may sound like exaggeration, but it is precisely what happened to me when I was still a young crook back in the sixties. How I got the money in the end and how I escaped without being detected are the things that this little reminiscence will tell. The robbery was committed many years ago, but this is the first time that anyone has divulged the way in which it was done and by whom. Without boasting, I think I proved that I was a pretty cool hand in that affair. At any rate it made my reputation in the underworld.

In the first place I got mixed up in the robbery through my keen interest in the manner in which safes are constructed. Even at that time I was a good deal of an expert in that sort of thing and had come to know as much as the safe makers knew themselves, if not a trifle more.

That was the era of big breaks, and along about 1865 the manufacturers vied with one another in producing safes each of which had its little run as "absolutely burglarproof." Safe-blowing with powder had been practiced for a number of years, and the crooks had invented tools which were highly successful. As a result nearly all the safes of older construction had been "beaten" at one time or another and considerable sums of money stolen.

At that particular time the best safes made were fashioned from iron and steel with plates superimposed alternately varying from three-eighths to one-half inch through. This arrangement gave the walls and door a thickness of metal of between two and three inches. As a matter of course the heavier types were used by the banks.

There was one especial "out" about these, and that was found in the way in which the door was hung. As a rule the plates on the door itself and on the jamb did not overlap one another, but were planed down to make a straight edge all around, after the manner of an ordinary wooden door.

A considerable number of these safes had been placed on the market, but their usefulness was soon brought into ill repute, chiefly because of the inventive genius of my old friend, George White, whom I have mentioned several times before. White brought into play a series of little wedges which readily penetrated the unprotected cracks and made way for the load of powder.

Naturally all the criminals of any standing had a keen interest in safe improvements, I among the rest. It was this desire for knowledge which led to my acquaintance with Shell Hamilton, a noted crook of that day.

Hamilton lived over in Williamsburg, opposite New York City, on Long island, and seemed to have an excellent reputation among some of "my friends, the enemy"—I mean the New York detectives.

These gentlemen on several occasions informed me what a fine worker Shell was, and that he was anxious to make my acquaintance. I was told that he had made a thorough study of combination locks, and that he might have information that would prove valuable to me. For a time I hesitated, but finally, after several envoys had been sent to me, I agreed to be introduced to Hamilton.

Our first meeting took place at his house, where we had a long talk about almost everything that pertained to our trade, but chiefly about combinations. I was pretty sure of my own ability in that line, and I soon found that Shell's ideas did not coincide with my mine.

On one point, however, Hamilton had some information which I thought might help me at a future time. This had to do with a new lock recently placed on the market and known as the "New Britain combination." This device had been invented by a Connecticut maker, and was more expensive than most of its kind, costing $300.

I had never seen one of these locks and when Shell offered to take me to a man who had one I agreed immediately. Accordingly, he brought me to a large machine shop not far away and introduced me to the owner under a fictitious name.

After some conversation, the man escorted us to his house and showed us the lock in question. He had asserted that he had discovered a way of picking the combination, so I was eager to see him prove it. Before he began his demonstration, however, we had to agree that if in the course of our work we ever came upon a New Britain lock and succeeded in beating it through the secret he was about to show us, we would pay him 10 per cent of any money that we obtained.

When these preliminaries had been settled satisfactorily, the machinist went to a closet and brought out the lock and an apparatus about three feet high, the principal feature of which was a 12-inch disc like the face of a large clock. Around the edge of the disc were marked numbers from 0 to 99 inclusive. The whole device represented an enlarged combination lock dial similar to those that may be seen on any safe today.

In the center of the disc was a movable pin which was provided with a hand like any clock-face. Behind the dial was a cog wheel connecting with the pin and from it led other connecting wheels which worked upon another wheel on the spindle of the clock.

While we looked on, the machinist began to manipulate the clock mechanism and from time to time marked down the numbers to which the hand on the dial pointed. After he had been at it for about a half-hour he opened the lock and showed us that he had succeeded in getting one of the four tumblers in the right position and that a second tumbler was nearly in place. There the lesson ended.

I was not much impressed and did not take a great deal of stock in the machinist, although he told us that he would show us how to complete the operation at our next visit and furnish us with a smaller mechanism for our own use which could be readily carried in a valise.

By this time I had an impression that the machinist's ideas about beating a combination safe were flighty and impractical. My own experience had taught me a better system than he had shown us but I saw no reason why I should confide in him. Moreover he appeared to me to be a man of a highly strung, nervous temperament and I could not figure how he could be a success when forced to work under circumstances which were the routine of the veteran burglar.

I understood perfectly well that any apparatus like that which we had seen would not be suitable for a bank-breaking job. Even if the lock could be picked, it would require several hours' work. I knew, too, that it was one matter to make the experiment in your own room in the daytime and quite another under the stress of a robbery. I did not believe there could be found a man with nerve steady enough to solve the mathematical problem involved at night in a bank with the possibility of discovery and the fear of the law in his mind.

Besides, in my casual examination of the lock in question, I had seen at once that there was an easier way of forcing the combination than that which the machinist used. I said nothing of this, but went out and bought a similar lock. I applied my system to it and although I was successful enough, in spite of all my bother I never once came across one of these locks in any of the banks I robbed.

I mention this incident because it indicates the care with which the old-time crook prepared himself for his work and also because it brought about an acquaintance with Hamilton which proved quite profitable to me later.

We did not go to see the machinist again, but in our walk from his place we passed an iron factory and machine manufactory which I had never seen before. A sign on the outside of the building announced that the enterprise had a line of safes as part of the business. As I had never come across the maker's name in my previous work, I decided to investigate.

Shell and I strolled into the place and interviewed the boss. He was a Connecticut man and had been in the business of making safes for only about a year. In that time, so he told us, he had sold several in his native state for the reason, as he explained, that his make was "absolutely burglarproof."

That claim was an old one, but if there were any new wrinkles in manufacturing I wanted to know them. I pretended that I might be a purchaser, and in his eagerness to sell me his goods he gave me very foolishly a list of all his customers, so that I might get satisfactory references. In the list I found the National Bank at South Norwalk.

On looking over his wares I saw that he did have, as a matter of fact, an improvement on the older methods. This particular device, he claimed, would prevent the driving of wedges between the door and the jamb, and thus make it impossible to blow in enough powder to wreck the safe.

It was a good idea if it had been properly carried out, but I was not long in discovering that there was a defect that rendered the whole thing valueless if attacked by a really skilled operator. The man was an enthusiast of the most pronounced type, and if I had told him there and then that I could beat his safe without difficulty, I believe he would have pronounced me crazy. Of course I made no comment, but determined to use his list as soon as it was convenient.

Only a few days later I started out on a trip through the Nutmeg state, and the first bank I came to was the National Bank of South Norwalk. At that time the bank building stood in the midst of a considerable lawn, set apart from the surrounding buildings. On one side there were some stores, while on the other side, across the street, was a hotel. The section was just on the edge of the business portion of town.

Before I made any plans I took the precaution to visit the bank during working hours and made as thorough an examination as I could of the premises, the location of the bank rooms, the position of the vault and how the safe was placed. From the counter where I stood I saw the open vault door and the safe inside.

While I was prospecting around I tried to discover whether a clerk or watchman slept in the bank at night. That, to be sure, was not a usual custom at that time, for the bank authorities had yet to learn from experience or from the advice of police how essential it was to have a guardian of some sort about after business hours.

Although I did not expect to find the place watched, I determined to make sure on that point at the outset in order to avoid future complications. With that in view I planted myself behind a hedge on the lawn of a private house across the street. From 11 o'clock at night until almost dawn I was wide awake to observe any movements in or about the bank.

During the earlier part of the night I had taken my station near the center of the town to get a clear idea of the regular movements of the police and of those who kept late hours in the town. While I was watching the bank only one watchman came past, at about 11:30 o'clock.

There was one circumstance which particularly attracted my attention, and that was a light which was kept burning in the hotel until early in the morning. The lighted room was situated at the rear of the hotel office and on the side nearest to the point where I was concealed. I kept any eye on the hotel as well as the bank, and at about 2 AM I saw two men leave the place and noticed that the light went out a little after that.

It did not take much penetration to understand that there had been a quiet little card game in progress in the hotel. I guessed that at once, and later events proved my guess correct. I surmised that the game was played every night, and so took that into consideration in planning my campaign.

To make doubly sure that no one went the bank at night, I had "tricked" the door early in the evening so that if it had been opened I could have told at once. After my long vigil I went to the hotel and had breakfast and then waited around until I saw one of the clerks open the bank door and go in. That was the first time the door had been disturbed since the night before.

When I was satisfied that there was an excellent opportunity to do a successful job on the bank, and after having secured all the needed details in relation to the building and the town, I returned at once to New York, placed the whole matter before Shell Hamilton and asked him to join me.

As we needed a third man to act as outside guard during the robbery, I called in "Little Dick" Moore, but to my surprise, when I told him the facts, he replied that he had already engaged to go with George White and some other crooks to rob the very same bank.

Their scheme involved considerable rough work of the kind that I did not like. They planned to visit the house of the cashier at night, to take him from his bed and to force him to with them to the bank and open the combination. That struck me at once as a crude arrangement, and I determined to stick to my own plans.

I judged that "Little Dick" had been taken into the gang for the reason that he of all the men interested was the only capable "sneak." I guessed that his associates had employed him to clear the way for them, and I was not long in finding out that Dick had already been in South Norwalk with White.

It seems that Dick had already visited the cashier's house, found out the precise location of the cashier's room and discovered how many people would have to be held up in order to make the scheme possible.

Now I knew that the violent methods proposed were not very often successful. When a lot of people had to be attacked, there was apt to be a disturbance which might lead to a general fracas and a possible capture. Such work, too, required a larger gang than I liked.

Besides, I knew that both Moore and White would rather work with me if they could, so I told Dick to go to White and propose that he join

Hamilton, Moore and me in the affair. I stipulated that White should get rid of his other associates and also that he should furnish the tools required.

White agreed at once to my terms and on a winter night in 1868 all four of us went to South Norwalk by train. We arrived at about 10 o'clock and scattered immediately, arranging to meet again later.

It was midnight when we gathered near the bank and began preparing for the break. Everything was still about the bank, there was nobody on the streets and the night seemed well chosen for a successful job. There was one little thing which worried me quite a bit and that was the fact that the light which I had observed on my previous visit was burning again in the side room of the hotel across the street.

I did not care to take a chance while there were men still awake and so close at hand, and for that reason we put our work off for an hour in expectation that the poker game would soon break up.

Just here I want to explain a circumstance in connection with safe blowing that every experienced crook had to guard against. I mean that it is never well to touch off a fuse while there is anybody nearby who is fully conscious.

It is a curious fact which I have observed very often when that a person is aroused suddenly from sleep, he never knows precisely what awakened him. Thus if a burglar should disturb a sleeper by blowing a safe close at hand, the sleeper would know that something had happened but he would have no definite idea of just what that thing was.

With people who are awake the matter is entirely different. A man possessed of all his senses knows an explosion the minute it occurs and can judge fairly well its locality. Now I knew that I would have to blow the bank vault and safe and as likely as not the concussions would be heavy. For that reason I did not like the poker party across the street.

After an hour had elapsed and the light still continued to burn in the hotel, I decided that if we were to do the job at all we would have to do it without regard to what might happen. Still I saw that we would have to be unusually careful.

I gave up the plan of forcing the front door and turned my attention to a window at the rear of the building. While we had been waiting, "Little Dick" scouted about and secured a ladder, and by this means I mounted to a little window over the vault.

Once inside I found a stairway leading down to the main floor of the bank. I had already concluded as a result of my previous visit that the place was not wired with an electric alarm, but I examined everything to make sure before I proceeded.

As soon as I was convinced, I unbolted the side door and went out. There I met "Little Dick," who reported that the light was still in the hotel window. To protect the gang, I detailed Dick on a mission to climb the fence, place himself close to the hotel window with the idea of listening to what was going on there and also of noting whether the blows of our hammering could be heard by the card players.

Shell Hamilton was appointed outside man with instructions to give White and myself the "office" as soon as anybody hove in sight. We were then in readiness to go ahead, but before we set to work we first covered the large front window with a black cloth which I had had made in New York for just that purpose.

It should be remembered that the safe and vault we were about to attack were of the improved sort that had been shown us by the Williamsburg maker, and were in some respects new types for White and for me.

As I have said before, most of the strongest safes then made had a straight jamb into which the door fitted. On that sort of safe it was comparatively easy to drive in wedges between the jamb and the door, and thus force an opening for the charge which was to be fired.

The improvement in this instance lay in the fact that the door jamb had been constructed with a crook or bend, so that a half-inch plate overlapped the jamb. The device brought the curve of the plate directly in the path of the entering wedge, so that it could be driven in only a half-inch and no more. A crevice of the slight depth would not permit the blowing in of sufficient powder to be of any service.

I had observed when I had visited the shop of the Williamsburg maker that so far as his vault doors were concerned the overlapping top plate did not overlap at the bottom of the door, but that the door rested flush on a sill forming a step. I knew, however, that the overlapping plate arrangement extended on all sides of the safe door, and to get the better of that device I was prepared with the proper tools.

As to the vault door, I had no particular fear of difficulty. As it rested on a sill, all I had to do was to drive in one of White's wedges between the bottom and the sill and thus force it up about one-quarter of an inch. Into this opening between the inner and the outer vault doors I blew a pound of gunpowder and then jammed in a length of fuse, leaving one end sticking out. I then knocked out the wedges and allowed the door to settle back on its sill again.

As everything was now ready for the first explosion, White and I went out to see how the land lay. We found Hamilton, who said that everything about the bank and the streets nearby was quiet. We then crossed the street to find "Little Dick." There the report was not so encouraging, as Dick said that the men were still playing, and that he could hear their talk distinctly, as well as the clicking of the chips on the table.

Although I realized the danger, I told Dick that I was going to let off the "puff" anyway, and that his part in the affair was to stay by the window, and as soon as he heard any of the men get up to leave to rush across to the bank and give us the word.

After lingering a minute to look up and down the street for any late pedestrians, I went back into the bank, touched off the fuse and left by the side door to join White and Hamilton.

A few seconds later there came a dull, heavy roar like the sound of a muffled clap of thunder. It shook the ground under our feet and was followed in a fraction of an instant by the crashing of glass, as the shattered panes of the big front windows crumbled into fragments. Then came the rattle and clatter of the big vault door as it tumbled to the floor.

There was commotion enough to rouse the whole neighborhood. While we waited a moment, dazed by the unexpected force of the concussion, "Little Dick" came roaring across the street to tell us that the men at the hotel had thrown up their cards and were coming out to investigate. The words were hardly out of his mouth when the hotel door opened and we saw four men step out to the sidewalk.

After I turned from watching the men for only a few seconds I was surprised to find myself standing alone. My three companions had faded away like spirits and were even then as far down the back street on which the bank abutted as their legs would carry them.

It was certainly no pleasant situation. My first impulse was to save myself at all costs, but then it flashed through my mind that I had gone to a whole lot of trouble and had put in too much hard work to give up just at that critical time. There was the bank vault no doubt filled with valuable loot, and if I left the neighborhood there was nothing to prevent the first passerby from walking in and taking the fruits of all my labor without anyone being the wiser.

In less time than it takes to tell it I had made up my mind that I would stick where I was until the last trick was turned. While I lurked in the darkness, watching with breathless interest, the four men stood across the street without moving. I don't know whether they were afraid, whether they lacked the initiative to act, or whether they feared that their little poker game might be discovered to the scandal of the community, but at any rate they did not seem particularly eager to uncover just what happened.

Although it would seem natural that they should think of the bank first of all, not one of them approached the building, and from where I crouched concealed I could hear them arguing pro and con as to what the noise might be. In the end they settled the whole matter on the argument basis and after 10 minutes of talk they seemed relieved when they came to the unanimous conclusion that a steam boiler had exploded somewhere. They were content to let it go at that. Then they went back to the hotel.

I waited 10 minutes longer and then went off scouting for my timid partners, keeping my ears alert for any assembling of citizens. I came upon White, Moore, and Hamilton some blocks away and it was only after considerable persuasion that I induced them to go back with me to the bank.

At last I overcame all their objections and all four of us hastened to the scene of our activities. We posted Dick outside the hotel as before, designated Hamilton outside man, and then White and I went inside to see what damage the explosion had done. At first I could find no trace of the vault door, but after hunting around a bit I came upon it at the other end of the room leaning half against the wall under the big front window.

The second vault door was still on its hinges but had been forced open. The vault was lined with a number of small tin boxes used by customers of the bank and out of these we sorted out more than $60,000 in United States government bonds. We placed the securities in a bag and passed them out to Shell Hamilton to guard while we continued to work.

There still remained the so-called burglar-proof safe to beat. In nearly all details its door was similar to that of the vault except that the plate overlapped the jamb and had to be cut away before we could get a place to drive in our wedges.

White and I closed the vault door and then I went to work with a chisel and hammer to chip off a length of about eight inches of the overlapping plate. Fortunately for me the plate was made of iron and not steel, but for all that it took me a good half hour before I succeeded in finishing the job.

At last I had cleared away enough of the plate so that I could drive in the wedges. It was no easy task as I had to hammer every one of the six that I used in rotation until at last the edge of the door was forced about a quarter of an inch from the jamb. I then blew in the powder and attached the fuse.

White then went out to call Dick over to our side of the street so that we would all be ready for a quick getaway. Dick reported that the card game was over and all lights out for the last half-hour.

It was now nearly 5 o'clock and those were the days of early rising, so that it was not the least daring part of the whole job to blow a safe at that hour. We knew, however, that there was a train for New York nearly due and we trusted that we could catch that and then make good our escape.

I hurried back into the vault, lighted the fuse and then came out, shutting the inner vault door behind me. In this way the explosion was muffled to a considerable extent and only a dull rumble could be heard. As soon as the smoke had cleared away sufficiently White and I rushed into the bank and quickly rifled the safe.

After we had crammed the loot into a bag, we left by the side door and the four of us set off at a fast jog to catch the train. There luck was with us again, for we were just able to swing aboard as the engine pulled out of the depot.

That was perhaps the most fortunate incident of the whole break and probably saved some, if not all of us from arrest. There had been a light snowfall during the night so that we could have been readily tracked by our footprints and the direction we had taken would have been quickly known.

Then again if our getaway had been by some way other than by the train we would have had to show up from time to time to get food or to hire teams. The robbery would have been discovered as soon as the bank was opened, and possibly before, as the shattered front window was bound to attract the attention of the first passerby.

As it was, we avoided all these contingencies and were in New York before the alarm was sounded. We left the train at Mott Haven and scattered on different horse cars to meet again at George White's house in the evening. There we found that our whole loot was in excess of $100,000.

White and I took over the bonds of Moore and Hamilton at a discount, and after the usual 10 per cent was set aside for protection money, we split the boodle in four ways. So far as the identity of the burglars who did the job was concerned, it remained a mystery to the authorities of the Nutmeg state, and this account will probably be news to them if any of them are still alive.

I have always regarded the robbery as an excellent example of the value of a cool head in a tight place. The be sure the fact that the poker game was going on almost under our noses was something to try the nerve of even an old-timer, but I have often pointed out to my associates that even when the explosion threatened to set our work at naught, we still had a chance if we had clung together.

We were four men who knew how to handles ourselves in danger, and the chances were in our favor for standing off the first comers and getting away with the loot before the town could be aroused. It always takes time for citizens to make up their minds to act, and in those critical moments we were sure of securing the bonds at any rate. It was a time for deliberate action and not for panic.

I mention all that not by way of patting myself on the back, but because my conduct in that affair astonished a good many of the New York crooks as well as the police officials of that city who were in the secret. My stock in the underworld counted continually after that. As a bank burglar I was easily on the top rung of the ladder. It used to be the general impression that no job in which I had a hand could fail, and for that reason I was picked very often for the work that was the most profitable to be found.

8 HOW FOUR GANGS SOUGHT TO ROB THE WOLFEBORO, N.H., BANK

In the heyday of burglary, back in the sixties and early seventies, bank robbing, safe blowing and kindred crimes came to constitute something that was very like an organized business. A large number of men were engaged in this dangerous occupation, and not a few of them were of a high order of intelligence, were skilled in a difficult branch of mechanics and were enterprising and fearless to boot.

These crooks of a past generation were not greatly different in personality and in mental make-up from their more respectable fellows. Indeed, aside from their criminal activities, they looked, behaved and lived much like other men. They were moved by the same passions and desires, they were seeking money, and what money could buy, and in the long run were little unusual except in the methods which they employed to get what they wanted.

Naturally, where loot was to be had so easily for affair amount of risk and a ready display of courage, there grew up a keen competition among burglars. Individual gangs came into existence everywhere, and in the course of time these gangs frequently clashed over promising jobs.

As a result, just as is the case of rivalry in other fields, there was wrangling, jealousy, overreaching and treachery. Crook quarreled with crook, one bank snatched the prey from another, and individuals informed upon one another and put up schemes of which rivals were the victims.

Just as an instance of what I mean, I propose to tell of one case where four gangs were laying plans simultaneously to rob a single bank, all working without reference to and without knowledge of the others. Curiously enough, while the first three were parleying to see which had the prior claim, the fourth organization slipped in and carried off the booty.

Then, too, I recall another case which occurred somewhat later, but which is a good illustration of the competition of which I have spoken. In this last instance one "fence" arranged a robbery of which a rival "fence" was the victim. The thief then fell out with the man whom he had engaged to melt down his golden spoils and the police were called in. Strangely enough, it was bogus goldbrick that won liberty for the crook.

It will take no very deep thinking to understand that where there was all this interplay of interests there should grow up a system of graft upon which the crooks depended in a large measure to keep them clear of difficulties. The old prosperous days of burglary, however, have passed, and old methods, both in the underworld and among the powers that be, have changed with changing conditions.

When I look back over 50 years to the time when the country was in the throes of a civil war, I often wonder why it is that recent revelations of graft in New York City should cause so much surprise. To be sure, the manner of grafting is not the same today, but nevertheless there was plenty of that sort of thing in the old times. Human nature is no different at present from what it was then.

During the war the great prevailing passion of patriotism overshadowed all others, but while the bulk of the nation had its attention concentrated on higher things the situation was nearly ideal for the development of the meaner passions among those who had no interest in the fate of the country.

I do not know whether there is any satisfactory record of graft as it was then practiced, but much graft there was, even in high places, and much of it went unpunished in the stress of the war and the public anxiety as to its outcome.

The arm of the law, it seems to me, was paralyzed as a result of the multiplied duties which were forced upon officials everywhere. The machinery which would have been directed ordinarily against the crook was employed for other uses owing to the state of war.

As I remember the underworld in the city of New York during the war and for some years afterward, about every vice flourished openly. Dance houses and disreputable restaurants might be found in every block in the Tenderloin district of Broadway between Canal and Fourteenth streets, as well as on numerous other streets and avenues. The Bowery was, perhaps, the worst section of all.

Along Third avenue, in the district in and about Park row, and on lower Sixth avenue, there were a number of places of ill-repute. In Greene street and in many of the adjoining streets almost every house displayed the red light, and pianos and other instruments supposed to be devoted to music made the night hideous.

Gambling houses were plentiful. I remember no less than three of them in one short block on Broadway. There seemed to be a mania for gambling at that time. Everything was wide open. It was at about this time that the simple game of "keno" came into vogue and established itself broadcast in basements, cellars and out-of-the-way back rooms. The familiar call of "keno" could be heard in nearly all the side streets off Broadway.

Crooks of every type, high and low, plied their trade or sought asylum in the city. Of course, the most numerous were the pickpockets, who were content with whatever they could snatch. Next in order came the counterfeiters and their agents, the passers of bad money. These men had an organization which ramified throughout the East, and they were often the persons who tipped off the more desperate crooks as to where a likely job might be found.

Then, too, there was a large company of hold-up men, ranging all the way from those petty thieves who preyed upon the casual drunkard up through the scale of the highwayman. Burglaries for small amounts and large grew apace, and in this class there were many divisions, from the common housebreaker to the bank robber.

As soon as gunpowder began to be used to "beat" safes, safe-blowing increased at an enormous rate. In fact, by the year 1866 there was hardly a safe in any of the coal or wood yard offices or in other buildings set apart and isolated which had not been wrecked by the aid of powder. I was familiar with a single gang that blew three or four safes almost every night.

During the war almost any young man arrested "dead to rights" could escape punishment by enlisting in the army. Bounty jumping became a paying business for a considerable group of men. I know several who made fortunes by offering recruits as substitutes. These fellows received at times as high as $1000 for a recruit, and when the transaction was completed promptly found means of aiding the enlisted man to escape. The same thing was repeated over and over again on an equal division basis.

My old friend Adam Worth, later famous for the Boylston bank break, the theft of the Gainsborough portrait and of the Kimberley diamonds, became a bounty jumper near the close of the war, but by that time the government had become suspicious, and Adam was shipped off to the front under a strong guard. He was forced to desert in the face of the enemy.

I have never seen so many smugglers as I met in those years. Tobacco and silk seemed to be the chief sources of revenue. Sailors or men dressed like sailors walked openly about the city selling smuggled cigars, and even pack peddlers were able to display the finest sort of goods to the women of the underworld.

Many United States deputy marshals were appointed, and I knew that some of these were of a class who might be trusted to look after themselves. Indeed, it was among them that I first noticed a process of levying upon the crooks.

Organized graft as such did not exist at that time among the city, county or government police, but those among the police who were grafters had each his individual source for obtaining illegitimate revenue. I recall many cases in which pickpockets, smugglers, bounty jumper and others were "shaken down" by city, county or government officials.

As I looked about me everybody seemed to have money aplenty, and almost everybody with whom I came in contact appeared to have a graft of one kind or another. People who knew that I was a crook treated me with the greatest deference. Officials in high places and still rising invited me to make Sunday calls on them, and after the Ocean bank had been robbed one of them sent for me and suggested I reform, settle down on the money I had and marry his niece. I could not do that, as I had already a wife in mind and intended to reform on my own responsibility.

The conditions which grew out of the war produced a crop of intelligent crooks of all sorts, the more courageous of whom turned toward burglary on a large scale. These men gradually resolved themselves into groups or gangs, and during the sixties and seventies there were a number of these gangs.

The burglar gangs gravitated toward New York City, and in the course of time that city became their headquarters simply because they were sure of protection against all outside police authorities who presented warrants for their apprehension.

Such a statement may appear to be exaggerated, but it should be remembered that Boss Tweed was then in power, and to those who are familiar with crooked politics that one fact should be a sufficient explanation. Just how close the relation between official New York and the crooks was is indicated by the fact that a friend of mine, a burglar, was chosen to sail away with Tweed when he escaped from the sheriffs in New York. The friendship between the two classes was pretty clearly shown by the fact that the gamblers, politicians, sports, and men about town had adopted into their every-day vocabulary numbers of words and expressions from the slang of thieves.

Many of the crooks who were then my associates later gained national and some international reputations. Among them were such criminals as "Dan" Noble, Chauncey Johnson, "Dutch" Heinricks, George White, "Eddie" Hughes, "Fairy" McGuire, "Rory" Sims, "Dave" Bartlett, "Jim" McCoy, "Red Bill" Wilson, to name only a few. With the exception of

White and McGuire all of these had been in the criminal class before the war.

During the progress of the war their ranks were augmented by a number of clever crooks, notably Langdon Moore, Harry Howard, "Tom" McCormick, "Little Dick" Moore, "Billy" Porter, "Sheeny Mike," "Jim" Tracy, "Red" Leary, and "Jim" Irving. Every one of these men was known to the police and to their friends by some particular trait in his work and all were more or less notorious.

My own dealings with the New York police were peculiar. For some years I had kept free of difficulties and of the need for appealing to them. In the spring of 1865, however, I was arrested at my farm in Saratoga and taken to New Hampshire to answer to a charge of robbing the Walpole (N.H.) National Bank. Up to that time I had been to the New York detectives only one of that numerous class which is gathered under the head of "sport."

When I escaped from the jail at Keene, N.H., on the day I was sentenced to two years' imprisonment, I hastened back to New York City, and once there received a tip that the New York police did not "want" me and that I would go unmolested.

Six months later I was again arrested and taken to the New Hampshire state prison. I escaped again after serving nine months and again went at once to New York. This time the formalities were observed more closely. My friend George White decided that it would be well for me to go to the men higher up. Accordingly he introduced me to "The Big Four." That organization as the name indicated included four of the most influential detectives at police headquarters.

This same group was also known to the crooks as "The Ring" and so controlled the situation at police headquarters that no other officers dared to interfere with their activities. My acquaintance was virtually an insurance against arrest so far as the city was concerned.

In the following years while the sentence in New Hampshire hung over my head like the Sword of Damocles, I felt the need of making the acquaintance of a number of other detectives in New York as well as some of the other large cities.

Although I always preferred to work alone when I could, the nature of the various jobs I undertook often brought me into association with other crooks and in that way I came to know the different "mobs" located in New York. These gangs played havoc right and left throughout the country, but always in the end returned to the sure asylum in the city.

As I said at the outset the criminal gangs were in keen competition and often came into conflict on the same job. One instance I related in a recent story of the robbery of the railroad office in Springfield, Mass., where "Little Dick" Moore and I took $20,000 from a gang led by George White.

A somewhat similar case arose in the sixties in the robbery of the Wolfeboro, N.H. bank. The first in the field were Langdon Moore and Harry Howard, the men who successfully looted the Concord, Mass., Bank. Moore and Howard visited the place, forced an entrance, but although they opened the safe were unable to drill into the burglar-proof chest inside. They gave up the attempt for the time being.

This failure did not shake the confidence of the bank people and after they had had the safe door repaired they left things as they were before the burglary. The safe still tempted the New York burglars and in the fall of

1869 "Jimmy" Hope and a couple of his men made a trip to Wolfeboro to look the field over. On their way out of town they met a well-known "mob" of English crooks under the leadership of George White who were on the ground for the same purpose.

In the meanwhile the news of the proposed break had leaked out in New York and still another gang began to prepare to take a hand. All the men of all the gangs knew one another and by a curious coincidence members of each organization met by accident in a machine shop where tools were being made for all three "mobs" interested in the bank.

Naturally there were hard words and a spirited wrangle between all parties as to which had the prior claim. Things stood still for a while and then the toolmaker, seeing a chance for profit, reported the job to a fourth gang which went out and robbed the bank while the other crooks were debating.

There were three burglars in the successful gang. One of the trio was sent over to Fisherville, where he hired a team and drove to Alton Bay. There he rested for a day and on the following evening picked up the other two men who had arrived on a train from Boston and the whole party drove on to Wolfeboro, arriving in that town at 11 o'clock at night.

As the summer hotel was closed for the season, the burglars had no trouble in hiding their rig under one of the hotel sheds. All three then started for the bank. While one of the men remained outside to watch, the other two forced a side window leading into the bank room.

After the windows had been darkened so that no light could show on the outside, the two burglars set to work on the safe door which was not a difficult proposition. Two holes were drilled into the bolt casing of the door and then opened up into a slot. A jack was then placed across the door, the screw started and with a few turns the outside plate was forced far enough out to allow the bolts to be worked out of their sockets with a jimmy. So far the operation had been practically noiseless.

When the thieves came to the heavy burglar-proof box inside the safe they had a much more difficult problem. There they found a quarter-inch hole about one-half inch deep which had been drilled by Moore and Howard during the earlier attempt.

The difficulty then had been discovered in the fact that while the iron top plate could be easily pierced there was a steel plate beneath which the drill would not penetrate. The new gang tried to use the same hole for drilling purposes, but after a great waste of energy the burglars were forced to give up that method in disgust.

After some time had passed they decided to take off the drill braces and resort to the use of wedges to open up a seam in the jamb of the door of the strongbox. By inserting very finely pointed pieces of soft steel and driving them home with a heavy copper hammer the door was forced open enough to allow for the introduction of a half-pound of gunpowder with a proper length of fuse.

The fuse in question was homemade and consisted of a piece of yarn soaked in a past made of powder. After the powder had tried the fuse stiffened and was still slender enough to be passed through a crevice one-eighth of an inch wide. An ordinary fuse would have made necessary a seam a quarter-inch wide.

When all was in readiness one of the inside men gathered up the tools and took them to the team which he brought out into the road to await the last stage of the job. The outside man remained at his post and at his signal that the coast was clear the inside man touched off the fuse and closed the safe door to deaden the sound.

He had just time to take his place on the other side of the safe when the powder exploded like the booming of a cannon. The force of the concussion was such that it threw back the safe door and sent the top of the strongbox hurtling across the room. Money and bonds were scattered in every direction on the bank floor.

After waiting for the smoke to clear away the inside man set to work to gather together the loot and was jamming it into a bag when a signal came from the outside guard that there had been a "tumble" and that the break was discovered.

The inside man was one of those cool hands who ae not easily frightened and he reasoned that if he had a chance of getting away without the money he had just as good a chance of getting away with it. Without paying any attention to the warning he kept on gathering in the loot until the man outside climbed up and stuck his head in the window.

"Come out quick," called the outside man. "There's a dead tumble and the people in the house across the street are up and flashing lights to the watchman at the boat pier."

Sill the man inside lingered and when at last he had stowed away everything in sight, he walked out quietly and strolled across the street to the house opposite. He saw no lights flashing nor was there any sound or movement. It was just another of those cases of panic which will seize a man in an emergency. The outside man had keyed himself up to imagining things that had no basis in fact. I have had several similar experiences with men whom I left to watch while I was carrying through a robbery.

The trio were not molested in any way and by 6 o'clock in the morning were in Alton Bay 20 miles away. They reached Boscawen in the afternoon and after sending their rig back to Fisherville took the train to White River Junction and then to Troy and New York.

I have said that New York at that time was an asylum for crooks of this sort, and so it proved in this case. It was not long afterwards that New Hampshire detectives went to that city, taking with them the stable keeper at Fisherville from whom the team was hired, in the hope of getting some clue to the burglars. The New York police kept them continually on the wrong scent until at last they became disgusted and left for home.

Old crimes are not done with, however, once the first escape has been made. Years later the burglar who had hired the team was arrested in Rhode Island for a lesser crime. Then the old feud which had grown out of the clashing of the gangs came to life again, and a disgruntled member of one of the gangs which had been beaten on the job gave a tip to a Boston detective and the Wolfeboro robbery case was resurrected. The stable keeper was once more brought forward, and on the strength of his identification the burglar was convicted and sentenced to prison for 10 years.

It may seem curious to some readers that in recounting my past experiences I have given in the most cases, names, dates, and places, and it may have occurred to them that in so doing I was exposing myself and the men who worked with me to prosecution for crimes which have gone unpunished. I should explain that nearly all these robberies in which I took part personally or in which others whom I known were concerned have been outlawed.

In regard to the incident I am about to relate the situation is somewhat different. This affair was of a comparatively modern date and sufficient time had not elapsed to place the participants beyond the power of the law. In giving the details, however, I feel sure that I am injuring no one because all those who were actors in the case are now dead. I think the story is one of the most peculiar I have told inasmuch as it illustrates a phase of the crooked life that is seldom touched upon.

Back in the year 1890 there was in Woonsocket, R.I., a loan and pawnbroking shop conducted by a man who also dealt to a considerable extent in jewelry and antiques. That at least was what his business appeared to be to most of his respectable fellow-citizens, but to the initiated he was known as a "fence" who handled large quantities of stolen goods of the most valuable sort.

At the same time there lived in Providence another "fence" who was even better known to the crooks of the first class. It happened that the men had had frequent dealings together, and in one of their bits of business the Woonsocket man had over-reached his fellow-tradesman.

The Providence man was much too good an exponent of business methods to allow his chagrin to be seen openly, but he set to work at once to devise a scheme by which he could get the better of his rival. After thinking the matter over for some time he came to the conclusion that it would be an excellent joke and a telling revenge if he could bring about the robbery of this man who made his principal income from the spoils of robbery.

With this in view he enlisted the aid of Moore, who had long been intimate with him. Moore, of course, did not care anything about the dispute but saw a fine chance for profit. He agreed at once to make an attempt on the store of the Woonsocket pawnbroker. After he had secured whatever information the Providence man had he called in a fellow-burglar who was known in the profession as "The Kid" and sent him to Woonsocket to look the shop over.

Not long afterward "The Kid" returned and reported. He said that the store was situated in a business block through which there ran a long hallway. From the hallway there was a side door which led into the store and he thought that this door would make the attack on the store easy. The owner of the place, he said, went home to dinner at noon without putting his valuables in the safe.

Upon this report Moore decided to visit the place himself and with "The Kid" paid a call on the pawnbroker. He posed as a possible purchaser of bargains and also displayed a number of diamonds of which he had a quantity and discussed with the pawnbroker prices and values on precious stones.

During the chaffering both Moore and "The Kid" found pretty accurately what the store contained and saw that the goods were of no small value. They were able also to get a wax impression of the key of the side door.

All was now prepared for the attempt, but in order to make the loot greater, Moore conceived a shrewd idea which marked him as a schemer as well as a crook. He prevailed on the Providence man to sell to the Woonsocket dealer a lot of valuable stock so that the store would be more than usually well supplied when the break was made.

This part of the transaction was completed after a few months and then Moore was satisfied that everything was as it should be. Meanwhile, of course, he had made the duplicate key. On the day before the robbery "The Kid" drove over to Pawtucket and remained overnight waiting for Moore, who came by train from Boston the next morning.

The pair drove to Woonsocket, arriving at 10 o'clock in the morning. They hitched their horse under a convenient church shed on a street leading out in the direction of Boston and then hung around waiting for the noonday closing hour.

Both burglars were disguised as sailors. They wore wigs and had colored their faces artistically in ochre in imitation of sunburn. As 12 o'clock approached they took their position near the store and kept a sharp watch on the proprietor until they saw him come out, lock the door, and depart home for his dinner. To make sure that he had really gone to his house "The Kid" followed him for some distance and then returned to Moore.

The burglars then slipped unnoticed into the hallway of the building in which the store was located and had no trouble opening the side door with the false key. Each man carried a bag under his coat. After fastening both doors on the inside, they made a systematic tour of all the show cases, taking everything that could easily be carried. They found the safe combination set only at "half-cock" and it was no trick at all for an expert like Moore to open the door. That, too, was soon rifled of its contents. They gathered together a considerable quantity of gold and precious stones.

As Moore had dispensed with an outside man on this job, the two men working together inside completed their work in short order. Everything was placed in the two bags which Moore held while "The Kid" went out the side door empty-handed to make sure the coast was clear. At a signal from his confederate, Moore followed, and each, bag in hand, walked calmly through the streets of Woonsocket until they reached their rig, They drove off to Boston and reached this city without being molested.

A few days later, after looking over the loot and fixing an approximate value on it, Moore settled on a price with "The Kid" and paid him his share in cash. The latter departed at once for parts unknown.

Moore removed carefully all the stones from their settings and then hammered the rings, ornaments, and watches on an anvil until they were unrecognizable. When that operation was completed he sought out a man whom I shall call Blank, who had all the appliances for smelting gold and silver. Believing the man to be thoroughly reliable, he made a trade with him for the manufacture of the battered gold into gold bricks.

As the quantity of their loot had been large, there was enough to make several bricks from the rings, ornaments and trinkets. These were melted down in a crucible and the metal poured into oblong tin boxes set in damp sand.

During the smelting process Moore made sure to take away the finished brick at each trip, as well as all the jewelry which had not yet been treated. Blank was anything but pleased with this proceeding and told Moore plainly what he thought of his suspicious behavior. There was some friction as a result, and when settling time came Blank demanded a much larger sum than had been agreed upon. Moore promptly refused.

They parted, however, apparently good friends, and a few days later Moore received word from Blank that the latter had a good customer for one of the bricks and the prospect of further sales if the first brick assayed as well as expected.

Moore and Blank agreed upon a price as well as the place of meeting where the gold was to be turned over. Moore, however, was one of those fellows who always carried his thinking cap on his head instead of in his pocket, and when he considered the whole affair he came to the conclusion that the proposition might be a "frame-up" on the part of Blank.

With this in mind he set to work to construct a bogus brick out of chunks of iron and melted lead, framing it in a tin box and carefully gilding the top. It was this substitute that he carried with him when he went to meet Blank and his prospective customer at the stated place in the hallway of a building on Tremont street in this city.

As Moore walked into the hallway he saw Blank and the customer standing near the door. Blank drew Moore farther back until they had halted opposite another door which led into one of the offices. The customer began fumbling in his waistcoat pocket, and after a little drew out a large roll of bills. Moore displayed his package all done up neatly in a wrapper, tied with a cord and sealed properly with wax.

The trade was about to be made when the door of the office opened and two Boston detectives stepped out of the room. They placed the whole party under arrest and without more ado escorted the three men to police headquarters.

Moore was not at all abashed and when the charge was being entered against him at the desk he remarked smiling: "Gentlemen, hadn't you better examine the property found on me before going any further?" As soon as this was done there was a look of disappointment on every face except that of Moore. When the wrapper was removed there was the slightly gilded mass of iron and lead. Moore grinned as he walked away a free man.

9 WHEN REVOLVERS BARKED IN A FAMOUS OLD-TIME HOLD-UP

I have seen my share of gun play, I have heard the revolvers barking all around me, and when the bullets were singing I contributed in my time some few selections to the concert. That doesn't mean, however, that I ever liked that sort of thing. As a matter of fact, I did not.

I do not want to give the impression that I was afraid. When it comes to fighting, I suppose, there is nothing to do but fight. Still, it always seemed to me that when a promising burglary wound up with shooting, somebody had blundered and blundered badly.

I think I have remarked in the course of other reminiscences that I disliked violence, and seldom went into work where force was necessary. That was due, I believe, to the fact that I came into the world with a plentiful supply of common sense. I figure that I was given a brain to think with, and I have always believed, and still believe, that it is the business of my brain to save my skin.

When I had a job in hand I made it a point to plan out my campaign in all its details. I had not been long in the business before I realized that there was something like a science in robbing banks. I trained myself in ways and means. I became a student of safes, and I think I can say without boasting that I was a mechanic of more than usual skill. I could work alone if need be, and I soon saw that half of the success came from not taking chances.

I call attention to these facts by way of contrast. There were other bank burglars who used other methods and came to grief through them. For instance, there were the hold-up men who went about in god-sized gangs, who relied on the fear they inspired as their chief asset, and who believed that mere dare-devil tactics were the surest aids to turning a trick.

I do not say that the ways of the desperadoes never brought results, for at times they did, but I do say that the same results might have been accomplished quietly and safely without making every affair something like the finale of a Wild West show.

Just by way of illustration, I mean to relate one of the early crimes of the first notable gang of hold-up men that ever ventured on a bank robbery. Almost every man in the band was a crook of reputation, yet after getting away with $300,000 four out of the six men were lodged in prison, one man had his arm shot away and the other one escaped only by the narrowest margin, and after an experience that most people could not contemplate without a shiver.

As I have shown in my previous stories, there were many ways of robbing a bank. Each had its advantage, but what the advantages of the hold-up method were I have never been able to satisfy myself.

It will be recalled that in the robbery of the St. Catherine's bank in Canada, which yielded $240,000, the job was done partly by means of wax impressions of safe and vault keys and partly by means of a powder explosion. The affair required only two men, and proved profitable, to say the least.

In the case of the $300,000 looting of the Concord (Mass.) Bank two men, by a simple display of persistency, carried the whole thing through without any peril to themselves or others only by securing the vault and safe keys, which were left carelessly in the bank.

To be sure, there were four men in the South Norwalk Bank robbery, but that was only because four men had to be taken in. That case was skillful in that both the outer and inner vault doors were blown open by a single charge of powder. The break was successful, and gave the participants a share in $100,000.

These few examples should be sufficient to show how a really capable crook achieved what he set out to do, and I have quoted them chiefly to prove my contention that the hold-up scheme was as unnecessary as it was foolish and perilous. Hold-up robberies, however, flourished to a considerable extent, and no history of the underworld as it was when I was young would be complete without reference to them.

It was in the spring of 1866 that the first gang of hold-up bank burglars came into existence. There were six members at the outset, and a more remarkable group I have never come into contact with.

While I was never associated in any way with this gang, I took a keen interest in its activities owing to the fact that my old friend, George White, threw in his fortunes with them. White had been charged with being my pal in the break of the Walpole (N.H.) Bank, and had been arrested and sentenced with me. He managed to escape from jail and went at once to New York, where a friend of mine made him known to some of the most accomplished criminals of the time. White, by the way, had been a man of business before he became a crook.

Besides White the gang included "Eddie" Hughes, a crook of years' standing, reputed to be absolutely fearless; "Red Bill" Wilson, another burglar of some note as a worker, but not long on good judgment; "Big Bill" McDavit, a man of huge bulk and the strongest I have ever known; "Jack" Utley, man about town, gambler and gentleman sport, as well as a crook of reputation; and last, but not least, "Tall Jim" Boyle, son of wealthy parents, a burglar for excitement's sake, and later the heir to a considerable legitimate fortune.

With the exception of White, who was then a novice, every one of the gang had a reputation for reckless daring, and when the underworld heard of the new fellowship nobody doubted that if there was rough work to be done these were the men who would do it without fear or favor.

As to the plan which they perfected, there was more chance for a display of brawn than brain in it. It was as simple as it was desperate. The scheme as it was perfected was, in brief, this: The members of the gang were to find promising banks, investigate the surroundings and then find out where the cashier lived. When those preliminaries had been attended to, the full band was to assemble and attack the cashier's house at night. They were to force an entrance, bind and gag all the inmates of the house and either compel the cashier to give them his keys or to so intimidate him that he would go with them, open the bank and place the treasures at their disposal.

After several consultations in New York City, where they made their headquarters, the robbers were at last ready to act. "Big Bill," "Eddie" Hughes, "Tall Jim," and White were sent to Pittsburgh, and from that point dispatched through the neighboring country to scout. They had orders to the effect that as soon as one of them found a likely prospect he was to telegraph at once the others, so that all six might work together.

At the outset "Tall Jim" took the lead, and when the scouts returned from their first trip and were reunited in Pittsburgh, he selected a small bank at Wellsburg, a little town in Brooks county, W.Va., as the one which seemed the easiest to loot.

The town lay several miles below Steubenville, O., on the left bank of the Ohio river. The gang took the train to that place and then walked along the railroad track to a point opposite Wellsburg. There "Tall Jim" and his companions stole a boat, crossed the river, and hid themselves in a thick clump of woods about a mile from town. While the others loafed away the afternoon "Tall Jim" and Hughes visited the town to look over the ground.

It had been agreed meanwhile that in the actual attempt on the bank Hughes, on account of his experience and known courage, was to be the leader. He surveyed his prospective campaign with no great delight, for the bank was by no means as easy as he had been led to expect.

The building was a single-story affair of stone, and was as solidly constructed as an arsenal. Indeed, it was evidently designed during the guerilla days of the civil war, and looked capable of standing a siege from without. The great door was of oak, heavily ironed on the inside, while the windows were protected by heavy iron shutters.

Hughes and "Tall Jim" were not long in discovering that if they hoped to win they would have to employ strategy and not force. In the course of their investigations they learned that there was a husky watchman on guard at night, and, while that added a new difficulty, they decided to make him the center of their plan.

They had observed that nearby was a gashouse, the watchman of which was a one-armed man, and they also noted that he and the watchman of the bank were much together in the early evening and appeared to be chums.

As soon as the crooks had abandoned all hope of forcing an entrance into the bank building they turned their attention to the gashouse watchman. They gang figured that he would be easy to capture, and they believed that they could force him to persuade the bank watchman to throw open the bank door. After that the rest would only be a matter of a scuffle.

It happened that at about this time that particular part of the country had been terrorized by bands of "white caps" and night raiders, so that it occurred to the New York crooks that they would do well to adopt the white robes and headgear of this type of desperado.

Accordingly the ghostly sextet set out to visit the one-armed watchman shortly after 11 o'clock at night. The moon was shining brightly, but that did not deter the robbers, as the town had been sleeping soundly for at least an hour.

They had little difficulty in capturing their victim, who was nearly paralyzed with fright. When he had been reduced to an abject state by threats he was taught his part in what was to follow. He was told that he must pretend to have injured his hand and that he was bleeding to death.

After he had been securely handcuffed the poor fellow was marched off to the bank, with Hughes on one side and "Tall Jim" on the other. He kicked at the door, and while his captors prompted and urged him on in menacing whispers, he begged long and earnestly with the bank watchman to let him in and give him aid.

The bank watchman, however, had received positive orders that under no circumstances was he to open the door during the night. Despite the pleadings of his friend he remained obdurate.

"Bill," begged the one-armed man in momentary fear of death from another source, "Don't you hear me? I've smashed my hand and I'm bleeding to death. For heaven's sake open the door."

Bill was not to be moved, even by that entreaty. The door remained closed. After waiting a few minutes longer the "white caps" gave up the attempt, and when they had led the one-armed watchman back to his gashouse and warned him not to stir until morning, they left the town as quickly as they could.

Greatly disgusted at the ill success of their first plan, they re-crossed the river, retraced their steps toward Steubenville and encamped in the woods on the border of that place. After one of the gang had brought in provisions and the party had breakfasted, they lay down to sleep with a sentinel on guard.

The gang had left New York without much money, and funds were already getting low. All six saw that quick action was necessary, and, after a council of war, it was decided that they had better have a try at the bank in Cadiz, O., which "Tall Jim" had found on his scouting trip.

Without further delay they took a train to Cadiz Junction, 10 miles from Cadiz, which lay at the end of a spur of railroad. There they got out and walked the rest of the distance, going into camp again in a patch of dense woodland some distance from the town. As before, Hughes and "Tall Jim" were sent forward to scout.

They returned and reported everything favorable for an attempt. The first necessity, however, was some provision for a quick getaway. That problem was finally solved by the finding of a handcar, by which the robbers decided to make their escape along the railroad tracks in the direction of Cadiz Junction.

White, who had no experience in the sort of work in hand, was left behind in a shanty to guard the handcar, and the other five men walked into Cadiz not long after 10 o'clock on a Saturday night. They loafed about the place until midnight, when Hughes led them to the house of the cashier of the Cadiz bank.

Those were the days of simple locks, and Hughes opened the front door easily by turning the key with a pair of "nippers." He entered at once and was followed by "Big Bill" McDavit, "Jack" Utley and "Tall Jim" Boyle. Outside "Red Bill" Wilson was left standing on guard, ready to give the warning of approaching danger.

While the other three men remained standing in the front hall Hughes crept upstairs in search of the cashier's sleeping room.

He had little difficulty in finding it, and when he tiptoed in he could hear the steady breathing of the man and wife in their sleep. Close to the bed on a chair lay a pair of trousers, in the pockets of which Hughes expected to find the keys of the bank.

He reached out for the garment and was about to go through the pockets, when it occurred to him that he had better make sure that the slumber of his victims was not feigned. A quick flash of his dark lantern across their faces reassured him, but just as he was pulling the keys from one of the pockets, the cashier stirred and started broad awake.

On the instant Hughes was on the alert, and before the man could even utter a cry the burglar's strong hands had gripped his throat and forced his head beneath the bed clothing. The man struggled ineffectually and in silence, but the commotion awoke the sleeping wife, who sat up in the bed, screamed once and then fainted in terror.

As soon as the three men below heard the cry they rushed up and in a minute had the cashier pinioned and helpless. "Tall Jim" then lit a light. The four captors began a series of terrible threats of what they intended to do, and soon had their captive completely cowed. He promised to do anything the burglars wished if they would only spare his wife's life and his own.

Hughes, however, was satisfied that he had the bank keys, and decided he did not need the cashier in carrying out the rest of the scheme. Both the man and woman were bound hand and foot, gagged and left lying helpless on their bed. Wilson was called in from the outside and stationed at the bedside as guard.

The four other men then set out for the bank, where the final strike for the loot was to be made. The gang had learned the night before that there was a watchman on the premises, and as he had the appearance of being faithful in his duties, the burglars were forced to reconnoiter before entering the bank building.

Peeping through the window, one of the gang saw him sitting behind the bank counter with his back toward the door. That was enough for Hughes. He was now ready for the attempt. From what he had observed on his visit the previous day he knew that the bank door was secured by a lock and was without a bolt on the inside. Besides, before going to the cashier's house he had peeked into the keyhole to make sure that they key remained in the lock.

It was only a matter of seconds to insert the "nippers," turn the key noiselessly and open the door. No sooner had it swung on its hinges than three of the burglars had sprung in, vaulted the counter, and seized the watchman before he could rise from his chair or shout.

Against such odds the man had no chance at all, and in a trice he was tied and gagged. While Hughes stood guard over the prisoner "Big Bill" and Utley opened the vault and safe locks with the cashier's keys. The whole robbery was completed in a very few minutes and the cash and bonds jumbled into a satchel. In addition to these lighter portions of loot there was a heavy bag of silver coin, and that, too, was taken.

The bank was locked up again and everything was left as the burglars found it. The four men then hastened back to the cashier's house to free Wilson from his vigil. After warning the cashier that one of the gang would be left outside the house to watch, and that his slightest movement would mean death, the desperadoes hurried away toward the railroad track.

After a little their progress began to grow slow, for Jack Utley, who had insisted on taking the silver coin, was staggering along under his heavy burden. Hughes saw that this would never do, and he reached over, grabbed the bag and threw it, money and all, over a barnyard fence on the outskirts of the town, where some early riser would find it, and, according to his moral make-up, either keep it for himself or return it to its rightful owners.

In light marching order now, the band made a brisk dash for the shanty, where they found George White waiting for them with the handcar on the rails ready for an instant departure. It was a very few moments later when the six men with their loot of more than $300,000 were throwing all their strength into speeding the handcar in the direction of Cadiz Junction, 10 miles away.

Meanwhile the cashier and his wife lay helpless on their bed until their negro servant woman reported for duty at 5 o'clock in the morning. Like a good and thrifty retainer she visited the pantry first, and there she found everything in a state of disorder. That was due to Utley's voracious appetite and sweet tooth. He could not resist the temptation of a quick lunch, nor could he be persuaded to leave behind a number of attractive pies which he found on the shelf.

It was that misadventure which led to an early discovery of the robbery, for the negro girl set out at once in search of her employers. In a few minutes she discovered them bound and gagged. The cashier had no sooner been released than he hastened to the bank, where he found the watchman, whom he released.

While the cashier went to the house of the bank president the watchman sought the sheriff, and in a short time the whole town was aroused. In the meantime the section hands had discovered the loss of their handcar. As there was only one direction in which the car could go, a locomotive was pressed into service at once, and soon afterwards a large posse of constables, deputy sheriffs and citizens was ready for the pursuit.

The burglars had three hours' start, but had failed to make the most of their opportunities. As the locomotive rushed along the searching party kept a close watch along the side of the tracks for the missing handcar. Cadiz junction was reached without a clue, but there the posse learned that a handcar had been seen going eastward in the direction of Steubenville.

With a clear track ahead the chase was resumed, and a little further on, in the midst of a rough, wooded country, the missing handcar was discovered lying overturned beside the rails. Here the posse got out, and the men spread themselves in a skirmish line to look for traces of the fugitives. Their search was soon rewarded, for they came upon a number of footprints along the banks of a brook, and followed them across an open field to the edge of a dense bit of woodland.

They had not penetrated the undergrowth far when they came upon the smoldering embers of a fire, which indicated that the bandits had breakfasted. From there the track led to a large boulder which stood on the crest of a ravine, and here all traces were lost.

For hours the posse beat the brush on all sides without result. Every inch of the territory was gone over in a systematic and fruitless hunt. At times the hunters would grow tired, stop and then start again with renewed energy.

Meanwhile the robbers were close at hand. After leaving the first camp George White had discovered in the midst of the ravine a shallow cave screened by a thick growth of creepers. Into this the six fugitives crawled and lay packed like sardines in a box. All day long they lay in their uncomfortable hiding place, scarcely daring to stir.

Some 10 feet above them was the summit of an eminence from which the surrounding country could be viewed, and to this point members of the hunting party came time and again. The men in the cave could hear every word that was said by their pursuers, and the remarks were not of a comforting nature.

At last night came on, and the robbers left their cramped quarters and started off again in the direction of the Ohio river. It was a hard tramp through fields and woods, but at last they sighted the river. A little further on they struck the railroad again and plodded along hungry and footsore.

Finally Utley's appetite got the better of him again, and he left the party to visit a farmer's barn for a raid on the chicken coop. In his eagerness he fluttered all the hens, and the birds set up such a squawking that the farm people soon discovered his raid, and a new and unnecessary clue was thus given.

The gang them resumed its march along the ties until they came to a narrow cut. Here they stumbled in the darkness against a rope pulled tight across the tracks. Beyond there was another posse lying in wait for the robbers.

Fortunately for Hughes and his companions, just at the critical moment one of the watching party struck a match to light his pipe, and thus revealed to the fugitives their new peril. Crouching and running as quietly as they could through the darkness, they made a wide detour and came again to the tracks about a half-mile further on.

A mile more and the robbers reached a deserted hut in a patch of woods, and here Utley insisted he would not go a step farther until he had cooked his chickens. His companions were now nearly famishing, and they agreed, despite the danger that such a proceeding involved.

After a hasty meal they set out once more, and kept on until they spied a wooded hill to the left. They made for it, and soon found on its side a hollow surrounded by a dense undergrowth. Here they halted to rest. It was now near dawn, and the band determined to sleep out a portion of the day.

Before they went to sleep Hughes, acting as master of the treasury, divided up the swag into parts and handed each man his share. While one man stood guard the rest lay down to their needed slumber.

The ground above the wood was open and cultivated, and for this reason no danger was expected from that direction. From his position the sentinel could view the country below and quickly give warning of an approach from that side.

About 4 o'clock in the afternoon, however, the guard was surprised by a sound from above him and a little to the left of where he stood. Turning quickly, he spied a man on horseback, and in a quick whisper warned his companions. The robbers crouched low in the tangle of vines and bushes, but the warning had evidently come too late.

"Come on," yelled the horseman. "Come on with the guns, boys. Here they are, like woodchucks in their holes." The response was a series of shouts from every side.

Seeing how hopeless their plight was, the robbers broke cover at once and scattered off downhill diagonally away from the horseman and his posse. As the quarry dashed out into the open there came a rattle of shots, and the robbers fled along in the thick of a patter of bullets which clipped the leaves on all sides of them.

Every now and then the burglars would halt, turn and fire with their revolvers, and then speed off again as fast as they could over the rough ground. Beyond them lay another thicket, and it was this they hoped to win.

Before they reached cover again, however, Wilson was staggering along, his right arm hanging limp and useless, broken by a bullet. White was bleeding from a wound in the hand. These two hung together for a while, but at last were separated by the thick brush.

A little farther on White came upon Utley and McDavit again, and the trio made for a meadow beyond and forded a creek. Another hot burst brought them to the hills. Meanwhile Wilson fell faint from his wounds and was captured.

All this time the pursuers, who were familiar with the country, hung on the heels of the fugitives. Exhausted by their long tramp of the night before, and weakened for want of food, the robbers began to fag, and the posse drew nearer and nearer.

At last White spied the entrance of an abandoned coal mine with a deep pool of slimy water lying in front of it, nearly concealing the entrance. He knew it was no time to hesitate, and plunged into the mud and filth. He called to his companions to follow, but when they saw him wallowing up to his shoulders they lost courage and turned to run again.

Sliding and slipping through the muck, White at last struggled into the entrance of the mine, made his way some 50 feet further until at length he came to a bit of high ground. From that point of vantage he looked out a half-hour later and saw the posse lead "Big Bill" and Utley past as captives.

When darkness came again White made his way out of the mine. I have said that he was a business man, and this was shown not only by the fact that he had kept his loot with him, but because now he determined to go and get "Red Bill" Wilson's share. He knew that Wilson had hidden his plunder in a small satchel under a log at the camp where they had slept the day before.

Despite the danger, White retraced his steps, and when the night was well advanced found himself near the spot. He climbed a little way up the hill and then started a big boulder rolling down the declivity. As it crashed on its way there was a shout and several men rushed off in pursuit of the stone.

White was convinced that the plant had been discovered, and that the men had been left behind in the hope that some of the robbers would return to seek the treasure. That was enough for George. He left the place and set off again across country. It was after many miles of tramping and many hardships that he finally reached another line of railroad, on which he took a train for Pittsburgh, and thence for New York.

"Tall Jim" at the outset had been fortunate, and had passed the line of his pursuers without being hurt. On the following day, however, he visited a farmhouse for food, and thus left a trace which enabled the posse to come up with and capture him.

"Eddie" Hughes, the old campaigner, soon broke away from his companions and made off for the Ohio river without drawing the pursuit. He got across and made good his escape. It was a curious coincidence, however, that a few days later the nude body of a man was found floating in the river some distance below. This was identified as the body of Hughes, and for some time afterward it was generally believed that he had been drowned in attempting to swim to safety.

Each of the four men arrested was tried and convicted and each received a sentence of 13 years in the penitentiary at Columbus.

I knew all the members of this first hold-up gang both before and after the Cadiz affair. Hughes was already a crook in the middle fifties, and even at that time I had heard him spoken of "high grade" on account of his courage. After the Cadiz break, in common with most of his associates in the underworld, I believed him to be dead, and for that reason I was surprised not a little when one day two years later he sent a friend to me with a proposition which led to the robbery of the New Windsor Bank, near Baltimore.

Despite his experience at Cadiz he continued in hold-up jobs, and it was in one of these that he met his death. In the early seventies he went with his gang to hold up the watchman of a factory at Oxford, N.J., where there was a large payroll. With George White he concealed himself in the office to wait until the watchman returned from his rounds of the mill.

Just as he was entering the office the watchman was warned of his danger by the barking of a dog which accompanied him, and as Hughes raised his head above the counter behind which he was hiding, the watchman fired point blank. The bullet hit Hughes in the forehead and he dropped dead.

White fired immediately afterward, but the watchman had turned and fled. This enabled White to escape, leaving the body of Hughes behind. It happened that Hughes had borrowed the overcoat he wore from an actor friend of his. The ownership was traced through a tailor's tag on the garment and the actor was arrested, tried, convicted, and sentenced to 10 years in state prison for complicity with the attempted robbery.

When I first met Jack Utley he was living in St. Louis in the middle fifties. There I struck up a gambling house acquaintance with him. Both of us passed for sporting men, but neither knew until later that the other was a crook. He disappeared from the underworld after he had served out his sentence for the Cadiz affair.

"Big Bill" McDavit died only about 10 years ago in New York City. I had always a weak spot for him because he once championed me and licked a big fellow who had insulted me in a bowling alley in Buffalo. Physically he was the strongest man I ever met, but little of the strength seemed to have gone to his brain.

After what he did for me in Buffalo I gave him several trials as an "outside man," but he had an unfortunate way of seeing things that did not exist and almost always warned me of trouble when there was no trouble in sight. He looked the part of the popular conception of what a robber should be, but in actual performance he was a failure.

"Red Bill" Wilson lost his arm as a result of the wound he received in fighting the posse. He was a capable worker, but lacked a cool head. After he had been released from the penitentiary he lived for some years in New York, where he died in 1888.

George White has been frequently mentioned in other stories. The Cadiz affair was his initial job, but after that he gradually came to be head of a gang of hold-up men. He was a man of considerable intellect and had a natural bent for planning, but in carrying out his schemes he always needed a professional burglar beside him with courage enough to go one step ahead of him in time of danger. Few crooks depended on him in a crisis, but he was indispensable to them because of his industry, his willingness and ability to advance expenses. After the trouble at Cadiz White placed himself under the protection of the New York police and was never disturbed.

"Tall Jim" Boyle was the most picturesque of the six. He was one of the few men I have ever known to take up burglary for the fun of the thing. His father was well-to-do and his family a good one. He had an abundance of sand and was never afraid to take the lead when there was trouble brewing.

About a year after the Cadiz robbery White asked me to go with him to Columbus to assist with the escape of "Tall Jim." I was told that "Tall Jim" had won over a prison foreman and one or two guards and that his sister had hired a house nearby to be ready to hide him when he was freed.

I met the guards at the house of Jim's sister and on the following day one of them took me through the prison and introduced me to the warden and the foremen of the shop where the Cadiz gang were at work. I had a secret word with all of them except "Red Bill," who was in the hospital.

The guard showed me all I needed to see for the liberation of "Tall Jim." The attempt was, I think, as queer a proposition as I ever had to do with. I made the visit to the prison in order that I might be able to find my way around the tangle of passages at night.

It was planned to keep the night guard out of the upper tier of cells and in the cell corridor on the floor below during specified hours. Jim's cell was in the upper tier, and it was my task to scale the 25-foot prison wall, descend to a passage like a narrow street between the wall and the prison buildings at the rear. There I was to spread the iron bars of a window which led into another narrow passage from which I could go upstairs to the prison chapel.

That part of the prison was not under guard at night, as the prisoners were all locked up in the great cell hall. Once inside the chapel I was to advance to the center of the prison where there was a door which was used by the prisoners when they went to chapel. From tier to tier where the prisoners were kept there were stairways and I would have to mount two of these to reach "Tall Jim's" cell. I was then to unlock his cell and lead him out the way I had come, through the spread window bars and over the wall by means of a rope ladder. White was to wait for us on the top of the wall lying on his stomach so as not to be observed by passersby.

Duplicate keys had been provided for opening Jim's cell. I met one of the guards at the sister's house later and told him I was ready to do the job.

George had given me $1500, of which I handed $1200 to the guard, who then agreed to give me the duplicate keys on the following night.

The next day at noon I hung around the prison until the foreman of Jim's shop appeared. I accosted him and slipped into his hand $300, but he returned it again and said that the plan of escape had been given away to the warden and that the best thing I could do was to leave town without delay.

I waited, however, to meet the guard who had taken the $1200, but I could not get at him and thus White learned that he had been buncoed out of that sum and all the expenses involved. White, however, stuck to "Tall Jim" and later had him brought out, packed in a barrel on a truck, which was passed at the prison gate by the son of the contractor who hired the convict labor of the prison.

"Tall Jim" came to New York on my wedding day and four days later he was with the party who bade my wife and me good-by when we sailed away for Europe. He joined White's gang again in a number of jobs, but was arrested ultimately in North Carolina and returned to the Ohio state prison.

After he had remained there a couple of years, however, his father died and left him a comfortable fortune. Not long afterwards the Governor of Ohio pardoned him, and "Tall Jim," having had enough of burglary as a pastime, disappeared from the ken of the underworld, married, raised a family, and is living today, a very respectable member of the community.

10 MARK SHINBORN TELLS STORY OF HIS MOST FAMOUS CRIME

Although I have played a part in robberies far more difficult and far more profitable, that of the Walpole (N.H.) bank has become associated inseparably with my name in the minds of the general public and indeed has had a truly baleful influence upon my whole life. From my young manhood to my old age that single crime has proven a stumbling block in my path at every turn.

For that one offence I have been arrested three times. As a consequence of it I have been forced to break from prison twice under the most sensational circumstances and at last, after 35 years had elapsed, I was clapped behind the bars to serve out a sentence which had been all but forgotten.

Around the doings of Mark Shinborn in New Hampshire there has sprung up a mass of legends. In quiet communities of that little state I have been to the imaginations of the older residents a character of a sinister importance not unlike that accorded to Jesse James in the middle West. In and about Keene, Walpole and Concord there are a hundred and one tales about me, all more or less garbled.

A generation ago every citizen had his pet theory of how I made my two escapes and each had his pet scapegoat upon whom he placed the blame. Nearly a half-century has passed since my first arrest in April, 1865, and now for the first time I am making public the true facts of the case, which has long been famous in the police annals of New Hampshire. This account will clear up one of the favorite mysteries of the Granite state.

To begin with, the Walpole robbery was my first attack upon any bank in this country and it was the last crime for which I suffered during my long career as a crook. It may shatter some popular conceptions when I say that the theft of $96,000 involved was one of the simplest operations I have ever undertaken. I accomplished it in less than half an hour.

Far more unusual were the events which preceded and followed my arrest, as those who will follow this story to the conclusion may readily see for themselves. My two breaks from jail may seem extraordinary to those who are unfamiliar with the skill and resource of an old-time burglar, but to my mind not the least remarkable feature was the manner in which I held a whole town at bay with a revolver which would not shoot.

I think there is no other incident on record like that which followed my first escape, when I, sitting on a log at the edge of the woods, a fugitive, addressed a crowd of pursuers squatting before me on the grass to listen patiently to what I had to say before I vanished in front of their eyes.

The true tale has circumstances grave and gay, but the tragic side is best illustrated by the influence my crime had upon the life of an innocent man. George M. White, a prosperous hotel keeper of Stoneham, Mass., was drawn into the affair by treachery. His whole career as a respectable citizen was wrecked, his fortune wiped out and he was driven to seek revenge as a criminal. Later as George Bliss and George Miles he became a notorious figure in the records of the underworld, and his loot as a robber ran up into millions.

Although the Walpole affair was my first bank robbery, I was by no means a novice in crime. For 10 years previous to that time I had operated in many parts of the country as a burglar, and had already won among those who kept posted on the doings of thieves a reputation of being a past master in the art of entering houses and stores at night. In fact, I was probably the premiere "sneak" in the business.

In a small way I had been uniformly successful. Measured by my later lootings, my booty was small to be sure, but it was in no sense insignificant. In a numbers of cases my takings ran up into the thousands. I had made plenty of money and went untroubled by the police, chiefly because I was unknown to them on account of the fact that I had almost always played a lone hand.

It must not be supposed that I was a petty thief. Compared with what the ordinary burglar managed to get, my income was large. Still it came in the most part in driblets and not in the large amounts to which I became accustomed later.

Up to my eventful connection with the little town of Walpole, indeed, my largest single haul was $15,000, and that particular robbery is important in my future career for the reason that it turned my attention to bank work, and also because it led to my acquaintance with James Cummings, the prime mover in the Walpole bank case.

In the early sixties there was in New York a band of counterfeiters of a really remarkable influence. The members of this organization had control of a huge amount of bogus money, the manufacture of which kept pace with the frequent issues of paper money by the government during and after the civil war. These men had a system which was not unlike that of a big business and was designed to scatter broadcast throughout the eastern part of the country the counterfeit notes that flowed into New York from many sources.

To keep the false money in circulation the counterfeiters employed a number of agents, one of the cleverest of whom was Cummings. He was not a passer of "the queer," but simply a confidential representative of the New York dealers. It was his duty merely to distribute the goods among customers. His business took him to many communities and made him acquainted with shady characters everywhere.

I was acquainted with several of the New York counterfeiters and it was through them that I came to know Cummings. I was informed that he had in prospect a bit of burglary in a Pennsylvania town which required the services of a skilled crook, and I was not slow in getting in touch with him.

Following the directions I had received in New York, I went at once to the house of one of the customers of Cummings in a little Pennsylvania village, and there I waited until he should arrive. He came soon after and unfolded his plan. The job seemed to be an easy one and I agreed to go into it with him.

When this had been settled we set out late at night for a little place some two miles distant, and there Cummings pointed out to me the store which I was to attack and explained the location of the safe which I had to beat. I saw at once that what was required was an exhibition of my usual method of "sneaking."

Cummings had learned that the storekeeper kept the keys to the store and his safe in his room at night and it was my part to go into the house and steal the keys. That was not difficult for me, for I become an expert in precisely that sort of thievery from years of practice.

Leaving Cummings concealed behind a fence several hundred yards away, I crept up to the storekeeper's house, forced the door and entered. In a very few moments I had tiptoed into the room, taken the keys from a pocket of a pair of trousers that lay on a chair and escaped.

Without wasting time, I hastened to the store, opened it as easily as if it had been my own place of business, and rifled the safe of its contents. The whole thing did not take more than half an hour and when I came back to Cummings with the loot he was immensely surprised. He had never seen $15,000 earned so quickly. We walked back to his friend's house, divided the swag and before dawn I had taken the train back to New York.

Naturally the remarkable success of the trick whetted Cumming's appetite. He was eager to repeat the experience and instantly began negotiations with me to enter a sort of partnership with him. To be sure he was no burglar at all, but he had a fund of information which was even more valuable than skill.

In his wanderings through the country as an agent of the counterfeiters he had come to know about all the crookedness that lay under cover in all the eastern states. His customers were many and it occurred to him that he might constitute them a sort of bureau of tips.

It was he who originated the idea which later made the counterfeiting syndicate one of the most notable agencies of crime in the history of the country. His customers, most of whom were supposedly respectable, were well posted as to local conditions and from them he drew pointers as to where large amounts of money were kept and how this cash could be secured.

He was constantly in receipt of hints for prospective burglaries from many localities and he was quick to nose out possible profit himself. Cummings was no skulker. With him there was no need for concealment, for although to a few he was known as a bogus money agent, to most people he appeared in the simple guise of a salesman for a fruit and ornamental tree concern in Rochester, N.Y., where his parents resided.

When Cummings was convinced of my ability as a worker, he at once proposed that I shift from my old line of burglary to the robbing of banks. He told me that his customers had furnished him with information which showed that there were banks "down east" which could be plundered as easily as any store or house.

As a starter he proposed that I should accompany him on a prospecting journey through Massachusetts and New Hampshire to look over the field. Although I had not dealt in banks before, I realized from what he told me that the work he proposed was little different from that which I had been doing, and I agreed.

Not long after that we came to Boston. I took a room at the Revere House while Cummings put up at the Tremont House. I did not want to be seen in his company on account of the counterfeit money that he carried with him at all times. This was in the spring of 1864.

Not long after cummings asked me to go with him to Stoneham, where he had a customer and where we could hire a rig to take us to several other customers of his. These men, he explained, had news of several banks that might be of interest to me.

We stopped at a little hotel and when Cummings had transacted his business we procured a horse and carriage and drove about the surrounding country. I met and talked with several of his customers and instructed them as to the facts I must obtain in order to carry out my schemes.

Several banks were mentioned at that time, among them one at Concord, Mass. And one at Keene, N.H. After some days we arrived at Nashua, N.H., where Cummings left me to learn what I could about the bank in that place. Later I drove back to Stoneham, where I returned the rig we had hired.

That last visit was to have an important effect on my later career, for it was there that I first met George M. White, the proprietor of the hotel and later, because of that acquaintance with me, one of the most noted criminals of his time.

There was nothing crooked about White then. Indeed my only interest in him was to make sure that if I wanted a horse and carriage at any future time I could have the best he had in his stable. To him I introduced myself as a United states marshal named Wycoff, and I think he never suspected that I was other than what I seemed.

During the season I paid two or three visits to his hotel and hired teams from him for two or three days at a time. On one of these trips I stopped at Keene, N.H., and obtained wax impressions of the keys of the vault doors of the Keene Bank. Besides I revisited several of Cummings customers and gathered much valuable information about other banks, notably that at Concord, Mass.

I was preparing to go after the Concord institution in September, 1864, when Cummings came to me and told me that he had discovered a "soft job" almost precisely similar to the one which I had done in Pennsylvania.

He had ascertained everything that was necessary to know, and I did not hesitate to fall in with his plans. I made him agree, however, that he would look after the hiring of any rig we might need and to arrange the matter so that I should not be obliged to "shop up" to any of his customers. We then decided to meet in Keene, N.H. on a specified day.

In accordance with our plan, I had taken rooms in a hotel in that place, and one evening, as I looked out, I saw Cummings drive up accompanied by White. Cummings jumped out and then White drove off.

As soon as I had an opportunity to speak with Cummings "under four eyes," I upbraided him for bringing White to Keene. He explained that he had had important business on the way and had needed not only the carriage but a driver. This did not satisfy me, as I had no desire to have any third party about when a burglary was going forward, and declared the whole affair off until Cummings should see fit to obey my instructions.

Cummings left immediately, taking the train for Boston. As he had told White that he was to meet me in Keene, I went at one to the hotel at which White had put up and told him that Cummings had returned to Boston. To further rid his mind of any suspicion I engaged him to drive me to Claremont on the following day.

During this trip I secured an excellent idea of the surrounding country. After we had returned to Keene and taken supper with a relative of White's, we drove off again and next day reached Concord, Mass., where I left White and continued on to Boston by train.

I looked up Cummings at once and we rearranged our plans for the New Hampshire campaign. It was settled that I should make the journey from Boston to Keene by train where Cummings was to await me with a rig and drive me to Walpole, N.H., where the bank was located which I was to "beat."

At that juncture a curious coincidence transpired which made necessary the postponing of the robbery for some weeks. It had been my custom when in Boston to stop at the Revere House and at that hostelry I was considered a popular sport because, I suppose, it was my rule to be liberal in tips.

On my last visit to Boston I had bought a handsome, shaggy Esquimaux dog and had left him at the hotel overnight in charge of the baggage man. For his services I had rewarded the man more than usually well and thus made him my friend.

When I had registered again the man took me quietly aside and told me that on two previous occasions when I had happened to be at the hotel guests had complained of being robbed. As a result suspicion had turned to me and two detectives had visited my rooms in my absence and searched my baggage.

He told me that I was being watched and that I had better be careful. The latter advice was not necessary, for I knew that if the police had gone through my effects they must have found a pair of nippers and a picklock, two rather peculiar instruments for a simple traveler.

It developed later that the Boston detectives who were on my trail were "Cockey" Heath and "Billy" Jones. Neither of them bothered me, possibly because I had deposited a large sum of money with the clerk of the hotel for safe-keeping. At any rate I left Boston and returned to New York without being molested.

It was the latter part of November before I determined finally to make my attempt on the Walpole bank. Cummings was ready to go ahead, and, following my orders, went to Keene. When I arrived he was at the appointed place with a horse and carriage. We started at once for Walpole, arriving at 11 o'clock. After leaving the rig under a shed we began to look over the ground.

Although the robbery was to have such an influence on all my future life and give rise to such a series of sensational incidents, in itself the crime was one of the simplest in which I have ever had a hand.

In its details it was almost exactly similar to the looting of the store in Pennsylvania to which I have already referred. It may be interesting to note that in each case I arrived at the scene in the night and departed before daylight. Curiously enough, too, if I had been taken to either of these little towns afterward I could not have identified any of the landmarks.

Cummings acted precisely as he had done before. He took me first to see the bank and then brought me to the house of the cashier. I had my "nippers" ready and it was no trouble to turn the key in the lock of the front door. I made my way noiselessly up the stairs to the cashier's rom. I could hear the regular breathing of the sleeper as I entered and that sound assured me that I had little to fear.

Soft-footed I edged to the head of the bed and there found a pair of trousers. I stepped out into the entry again, fumbled in the pockets and drew out a number of keys. That was all I required. I replaced the trousers and left the house, shutting the outer door behind me.

At the present time it is difficult to conceive how ridiculously easy was the robbery of that bank. All that I had to do was to sort out the keys, open the bank doors and walk to the safe for all the world as if I were some official of that institution. The actual theft meant merely that I had to turn a key in the lock of the safe. Naturally I did that as quickly as I could, took all that was of value and then left.

From the time I had approached the house of the cashier until I was back in the wagon again with Cummings less than a half-hour had elapsed, and as a result of that brief period of endeavor Cummings and I were some $96,000 richer. Hours before the town had been aroused to one of the greatest misfortunes in its history, Cummings and I were driving off toward Keene again.

We arrived there in good time and I was lucky enough to catch a train in the nick of time for Boston. Just before we came to the city I alighted and then made my way through the suburbs and thence to the house of a friend, where I had a long sleep after my night's labor. On the following day this friend drove me to Providence, where I took the train for New York City.

I should explain that the robbery of the Walpole Bank had been the last thing in my mind when I first started East with Cummings. My program as I had marked it out called for the looting of a bank at Nashua, a bank in Keene and a bank in Concord, Mass. When Cummings mentioned the Walpole Bank it seemed to me so easy that I decided to "beat" it as a preliminary to my more serious campaign in Keene and at Concord.

I had the wax impressions of the Keene Bank already and had laid my plans for a successful attempt on the Concord (Mass.) Bank. It will be remembered that the latter institution was subsequently plundered by Langdon Moore.

As the matter of horse and carriage played an important part in what came to pass after, I call attention to the fact that our rig was hired from one of the numerous customers of Cummings with whom he had dealt in paper money. George M. White had absolutely nothing to do with the supplying of our conveyance and knew nothing whatever of the robbery of the Walpole Bank. The rig had been hired in the vicinity of Keene and the man who furnished it received several hundred dollars from the funds of the Walpole Bank.

White's only connection with Cummings came from the circumstance that the former kept a livery stable and had been recommended to the counterfeiter as a man who could furnish the best horses to be found anywhere outside of Boston. The Walpole bank was the personal find of Cummings and had been unearthed by him in his trips to circulate false money among his customers in the neighborhood of Claremont and Bellows Falls.

During the winter of 1864 and 1865 I lived like a lord on the proceeds of the robbery in New York City. When spring came I went up to a farm which I had in Saratoga on the borders of the town and busied myself as a landed proprietor by laying out an extensive orchard. I had purchased several race horses and these I had shipped to my summer place expecting to take a flyer on the track during the season.

Meanwhile I kept in touch with Cummings and learned that in the selling of some of the bonds we had stolen at Walpole some trouble had resulted which had brought him under the eye of the police. He was aware that the police were looking for him. During the spring he had visited my farm and had also written to me.

Shortly afterwards I went to New York and decided to call on him at his apartment in Williamsburg which was situated above a store. I found him, but when I returned again a week later my difficulties began. When I rang the bell the pretty wife of the storekeeper opened the door and as soon as she saw me she turned deathly pale.

Without a word she took me by the coat sleeve and pulled me into the hall. "Don't let my husband see you," she whispered, all the time leading me further down the passage. At the end she drew me into a little room and sat down apparently overcome.

When she had recovered her self-possession again she told me that Cummings had departed in a hurry a few days before and that on the following day the police had come and taken possession of everything in his rooms.

She begged me to go away as quickly and quietly as possible. I do not remember that I said a single word during the whole recital. I did not attempt to thank her then, but took her in my arms, kissed her and hurried away.

I hastened over to New York at once, found a friend of Cummings and learned that my partner had just returned from Saratoga. It was not long before I found him and then discovered that he had been drinking a few days before and had tried foolishly to pass a $10 counterfeit bill on the saloon-keeper. He had been promptly arrested.

At the police station several hundred dollars of good money was found in his possession but no other counterfeits. He told a plausible story, gave his name and his address and when the police locked him up they found everything as he said. He was released.

Cummings knew, however, that as soon as the report of the case was sent to headquarters the next morning, the New York detectives who were interested in the Walpole case would not fail to see the significance of the case and would come after him again. For that reason he lost no time in getting away from the neighborhood.

I had been fortunate in not being arrested when I visited him, but my intimacy with Cummings was already proving disastrous although I did not realize it. The outcome was the result of one of those fateful slips which mean so much to crooks when the officers of the law are on his trail.

Cummings, it should be remembered, was not a professional as I was and did not appreciate the need of watching every step. He had been in the habit of keeping me in good humor, as he supposed, by making me little presents to show his friendship. Among other things he subscribed to a number of papers or magazines which he placed at my disposal.

While his home at Williamsburg was under surveillance by the police the publications were delivered regularly at first but in the course of a few weeks the *Scientific American* ceased to appear. That fact at once caught the attention of the detectives, and went they went to the office of the publication they learned the subscriber had ordered it transferred from the old address to that of "Mr. Mark Shinborn, Saratoga Springs, N.Y."

The change was made in a spirit of kindness. But I was not aware of it, and the matter slipped Cummings' mind. In the meantime I had made an arrangement with Cummings to send to him some railroad bonds which were a part of the Walpole Bank property. These were to be directed to an address in Philadelphia, where he had taken up quarters after leaving New York.

As soon as I had returned to Saratoga, I took the bonds from their hiding place at my farm and enclosed them in a letter to Cummings at the address he had given. I was all ready to go to the post office with them and was on my way when I noticed that a minstrel show was just about to begin at one of the halls in the town. Instead of posting my letter I turned aside and entered the hall.

While I sat there enjoying myself, two New York detectives arrived in Saratoga. They had already telegraphed to Detective Case, a local man, to keep an eye on me, and when they appeared on the scene he was able to tell them that I was at the minstrel show.

When the show was over I came out with the crowd, but no sooner had I reached the sidewalk than I found myself surrounded by the three detectives. Two of them grabbed me by the arms while the third shoved a revolver under my nose. There was no use in resisting, so I walked peacefully to the lockup.

There I was at once searched, and the tell-tale letter found in my pocket. One of the New York men sent Case off on some errand or other and then opened the letter and saw at once where the bonds belonged. He saw, too, that Cummings was as good as caught. I knew one man by sight from my experience in New York. He and his partner had spoken to me once about a year before in an attempt to make my acquaintance.

While Case was busy elsewhere, one of the New York detectives spoke up. "Now is you time," he said, "if you have anything to say, before the other man returns."

As I was dumbfounded by my arrest and had up to that time looked upon the police as my natural enemies, I made the greatest mistake of my life. I refused to discuss the case. Before anything more was said Detective

166

Case came back and naturally asked to see what was in the letter.

I remained in the lockup until the next morning and then we went to New York by train. During the night my house had been searched and a number of burglar's tools found as well as the wax impressions of the vault doors of the Keene bank.

In the hours which I had spent in the lockup I had come to a realization of the seriousness of my position and was able to see the error I had made in not talking to the New York men. On the train I made them a proposition to pay them $5000 in cash and agreed to let them "stand in" on the future robbery of the bank at Keene if they would suppress all evidence and prevent my extradition from the state of New York.

My proposal came too late, although they both admitted that if I had spoken before Detective Case had got into the affair other arrangements might have been made. I saw little use in making a stand and when I was taken to headquarters in that city I consented to waive extradition proceedings and go at once to New Hampshire. I arrived the following evening at Keene in charge of New York officers.

The news of my coming had spread and when I arrived I was greeted by a great crowd eager to catch a glimpse of a great desperate bank robber. I was taken at once to the county jail. It was a forbidding structure, very strong, constructed of giant blocks and with its windows protected with a triple set of crossbars. There was a double set of iron doors leading into the cell corridor and the doors to the cells were furnished with a series of closely set crossbars two inches wide and a half-inch in thickness.

I was lodged in the second story in a large room, the floor of which was fashioned of granite slabs 8 to 10 inches thick. The jail was the strongest I had ever seen or heard of. At first there seemed little hope of escape.

I had not been long an inmate when Cummings was brought in by the New York detectives and lodged in one of the cells upstairs. An official of the bank called soon after and during a private conference with me told me that the case might be adjusted if I had the means to satisfy the bank. I knew, however, that I was not sufficiently in funds to settle as I had spent the major portion of my loot in lavish living during the intervening months. There was nothing for me to do but to refuse to negotiate.

For about a week thereafter I became aware that there was a great deal of wire pulling and log rolling in progress, in the course of which Cummings was taken downstairs many times for secret consultations. A little later I was surprised to see George M. White, the Stoneham hotel keeper, brought to jail as a prisoner and to learn that Cummings had disappeared.

This is the true story of the liberation of Cummings, a story that has never before been told. When his name had been definitely brought into the case through the letter found in my possession at the time of my arrest, the detectives had no difficulty in bringing him to book.

The letter contained securities known to have been stolen from the Walpole Bank. The next step, then, was to send them on to Cummings at the address he had given, which happened to be a Philadelphia express office. The rest was simple. Cummings called for his letter, received it and its incriminating contents, and was promptly taken with the goods in his hands.

Once under arrest Cummings was told I had "squealed." The game was an old one, but under the circumstances I cannot blame him for believing the story. He was convinced that I had given him up and therefore he made up his mind to save himself by any means that came to hand.

I have said that the counterfeiting syndicate which he represented was a power in the underworld, and in this instance its influence was felt. The gang had to come to his assistance promptly, for the reason that he knew their doings in detail and could make trouble if so disposed.

It was not long before the counterfeiters had raised a fund over and above the $5000 found in his possession to settle the case, and had made arrangements to have him liberated. In spite of this, however, the county authorities knew that they must have an accomplice to take his place beside me at the bar of justice.

Cummings then bethought himself of White, who had been seen in his company and mine on our numerous scouting trips, and White it was who was chosen to share the burden of the robbery with me. In dragging in White, Cummings managed to save his friend who was the dealer in false money who had actually furnished us with the team we had used in the Walpole robbery.

There was little use for me, a principal in the crime, to insist that White was innocent, even if I had been inclined to do so. I held no strong position myself. I was the active factor in the robbery, and had not the means to settle and had to rely on some other means of outwitting the authorities. Moreover my friends pointed out that the presence of White, a man evidently guiltless in the affair, would make my conviction difficult.

My chief reliance, however, was not in settlements or in the twists of the law, but in the fact that I did not believe that there was any jail strong enough to hold me whenever I desired to escape.

The preliminary examination was put off from week to week, but at last when five weeks had passed, White and I were arraigned as joint culprits and held in heavy bail for the action of the grand jury. In the meantime my friends were working hard for me and with such success that it seemed as if the New York detectives had been won over to my side.

It was at the October term of court that my case came to trial at last. I was placed at the bar and beside me stood George White, who was made co-defendant despite strenuous efforts on the part of his counsel to secure him a separate hearing. The taking of evidence lasted for a couple of weeks. One of the detectives who, I had thought, would be a favorable witness became confused on the stand and really spoiled my chances.

The jury found me guilty, but disagreed in the case of White. By that time my friends had rallied to my support in force and many of them were on hand. They were particularly incensed at the detective witness and were not sparing in what they said to him. The other New York man, by the way, had been strongly in my favor.

My friends insisted that my escape must be effected before I could be taken to state prison and as they were powerful in the underworld they knew just where to apply the pressure. As a matter of fact I was all prepared to get away and had been for several months. I needed, however, something that looked like a revolver so that once free I could intimidate the townspeople and check pursuit when it became too warm.

The weapon was at last forthcoming in the shape of an old revolver with a broken spring, so badly damaged that the hammer could not be cocked. As a workable firearm it was absolutely useless, but for all that it had a very businesslike appearance, and that was all I required.

I had some trouble in getting even this into my hands, for every attempt on the part of my friends to smuggle to me either in the courtroom or in jail was frustrated by the vigilance of my guards. My friends after some debate put the matter up to the detectives, and when they came to the jail to take leave of me the thing was carried through.

The detectives came to my cell to say good-by and while the jailer was talking to White who was locked up in an adjoining cell, one of them slipped the gun to me through the small opening in my cell door through which my meals were handed to me.

When I thought of the ten years of hard labor which lay before me in state prison I decided that no time was to be lost in effecting my escape. For some time past I had had keys for all the cell doors. There has always been considerable mystery about the way I obtained these, but the matter was really very simple.

It happened that the roof of the jail had been mended shortly before my arrival and that the yard was littered with bits of zinc. That was all I needed to know. I procured a broom handle and a bit of string with a running loop in the end. For some time I spent my leisure hours when not observed in fishing out my cell window and was rewarded for my patience by pulling up several small pieces of metal. It was no trouble to me to cut these into keys for that was a branch of my profession in which I had long been an expert.

There were two doors, those leading from the warden's house into the jail to which I had no keys. One of these was a blind door which could be only unlocked from the outside. This fact did not bother me as the keys would not be necessary for these under the plan I had shaped for my escape. The time I had chosen was 4:30 in the afternoon when my supper was brought to me.

To understand just how the trick was turned it is necessary to have some knowledge of the way in which the jail was laid out. This, I think, can be gathered best from the plan which accompanies this article.

It will be seen that White and I occupied the second floor of the jail. We were placed each in a light cell with a dark cell between us, the door of which was directly opposite the main entrance to the jail corridor. The corridor was at the head of the stairs leading from the jailer's house.

About an hour before I judged my supper would be carried to me I unlocked my cell door and slipped into the dark cell, leaving the door of that cell unlocked.

White stood at his cell door [letter A in plan] while I was placed at the entrance of the dark cell [letter X in plan]. The main doors were opened by the jailer's wife, Mrs. Wilder, and her daughter, Miss Wilder. Miss Wilder carried a tray on which was White's supper and mine. I was glad to note the absence of Wilder, the jailer.

The two women walked diagonally across to my cell door [letters O-O in the plan] and called my name. At the same instant I had pushed open the door of the dark cell and waving a silent farewell to White, I passed swiftly through the entrance door [A1 in plan].

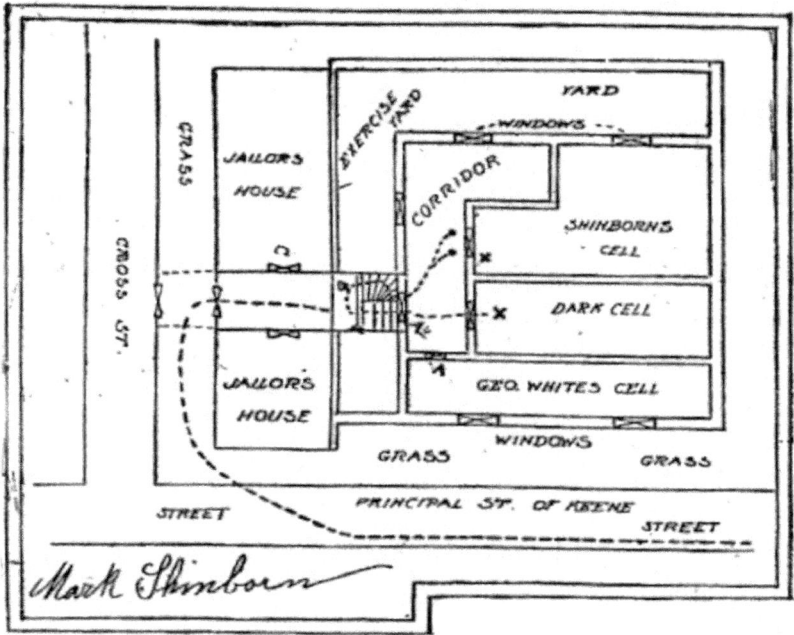

Plan of Keene, N. H., Jail, Drawn by Mark Shinborn, Showing How He Made His Escape.

Below me five or six stairs further down on a landing stood Wilder. He turned and looked at me in amazement and before he could recover I pointed my revolver at him. Without a word he turned and fled down the stairs while I followed close at his heels. Just then the women saw that I had escaped and began to scream.

At the foot of the stairs Wilder, still running as fast as he could, passed through the hall and into the living room. That was what I hoped he would do, and as he turned in one direction, I kept on in the other passing out the front door to the street and taking a course [marked by dotted lines in plan] to gain the outskirts of the town.

I ran along the sidewalk on the side of the street opposite to the jail. Meanwhile wilder had recovered his senses and had raised a cry for help.

The neighborhood began to buzz with excitement and I soon realized that the chase was on in earnest.

About a block beyond me I saw a man standing on the lawn in front of his house. As I approached he leaped over a low fence to the sidewalk and stood blocking the way. I knew that it was no time for parleying and as I drew up to him I pointed my disabled revolver at him. "Jump right back again," I ordered with a smile. He jumped.

My object was to reach the outskirts of Keene with all possible speed and then turn from the main street, bending my course to the right to reach the wooded hills which lay about a half-mile beyond.

Trotting along at a steady jog to husband my strength for an emergency, I came at last to a side street, a lone country road with only a meagre scattering of houses in sight. I turned into this, and as I paused for a second I could hear the hoarse murmur of my oncoming pursuers, whose numbers were augmented at every corner.

I was still well in advance, but the lead was by no means a safe one. As I turned again to resume my flight I was aware of a fresh obstacle. There directly in my path was a man, swinging along in a leisurely fashion, apparently undisturbed by the plight of the hunted or the perplexities of the hunters.

Across his shoulders was slung a yoke from the ends of which hung two large pails. At first I thought that I could intimidate this fellow as easily as I had the man on the lawn, but in that I was mistaken. For cool, solid persistency I never saw this man's equal.

As I edged up closer to him, he awoke from his meditations and spied the hue and cry in my rear. In the most deliberate manner imaginable he deposited his yoke and pails upon the ground and stood waiting for me without a trace of excitement.

I pointed my gun at him and ordered him to make way. He said nothing, nor did he seem at all taken aback. While my revolver covered his body and should have warned him of imminent danger, he kept hunching towards me, his left side thrust forward and his left arm gathered in close to protect his heart.

It was really a desperately tight place. I was winded from my long run and in no shape to mix it up with my husky antagonist; my revolver was as useless as if it had been a painted wooden popgun. Behind me as I hesitated the following crowd drew every second closer.

I renewed my threat to shoot, this time sharply, but still my silent opponent shuffled inch by inch nearer. I saw that if I could not make this man weaken in the space of half a minute it was all up with me.

He had evidently made up his mind to risk a chance of one shot from the revolver. He was now within six feet, drawing nearer and nearer. I retreated a step, raised the weapon to his head and concentrating all my mind to make my words carry home, I said in a level tone: "So help me God, if you don't get out of my way I'll put a bullet through your brain."

It was curious to look back at the spectacle of that man of undoubted pluck weakening before one desperate threat. His nerve was broken and he turned aside, stooping to the roadside to pick up a stone as I dashed by him. I could not resist the temptation of warning him that I could hit him twice as surely as he could hit me.

Beyond I came to a hill up which I walked to save my wind and there at the end of it was the wood I was seeking. Then occurred as peculiar a circumstance as I ever met in all my eventful career. The crowd at my heels had grown larger and larger; in fact, it had become now quite a congregation.

At the edge of the thicket I looked back and saw that not one of my pursuers was armed. I was young then and fearless, so that even in my perilous situation I could not help being amused. I do not suppose the thing could happen outside the United States, but I halted and sat down on a log with my revolver dangling carelessly in my hand. As I did so my pursuers hesitated and then took seats on the grass some 30 or 40 feet away from me.

It was for all the world like an open air meeting, and as they had come so far I could not disappoint them. I told them that I was bound to get away, that it was no use to follow me, and, most important of all I think, I convinced these people that I was a dead shot.

I had hardly concluded my impromptu remarks when I saw at the foot of the hill a party of sheriffs fully armed coming toward me. My congregation looked on expectantly and my last words were: "There are the authorities coming with guns. Please tell them from me that if any of them follow me into the woods where I am about to go I shall shoot to kill."

With that I turned on my heel and disappeared in the dense underbrush.

On the top of one of the highest of the hills I lay down to rest for a while to wait until it was dark. The moon shone out clearly and below me on the road I could hear many men talking and the rumbling of passing teams. I had to determine which route I would take, whether in the direction of Boston or in the direction of Claremont.

I chose the latter and at about 3 o'clock in the evening I started along the hill a struck the road about a mile and a half beyond Keene. The road wound in sweeping curves around the base of the hills and as I made a turn I came upon a man sitting on a milestone. As soon as I passed he got up. I faced him and called out, "Sit down again, sir, and you will see more and feel less." He sat down, and I walked around another curve out of his sight.

There I spied another man not far ahead of me. This was too much for me and I turned back into the woods to make a new plan. At last I decided that I had better break into some house and loot the pantry and was walking into Keene again with this idea in mind when I bethought me of a house near the jail where I had friends and might get what I needed.

I went to this house and knocked softly at what I judged might be the bedroom. A woman came and opened the window and I explained my predicament to her and asked for a pair of scissors to cut off my side whiskers, a hat and some food to carry with me. She disappeared and soon returned with the scissors and a brown slouch hat. I stepped into the woodshed and cut off my beard and then went back to the window where I was given a parcel of food.

Her husband spoke to me from inside the room and asked me if I was not afraid of being rearrested before I reached a place of safety. "With that bundle of food," I replied, "I can easily keep under cover and they will never be able to trace me."

As I turned to leave I kissed the woman's hand and said, "Madam, I thank you with all my heart. I have no way of expressing my gratitude to you, but I am certain that your little girl will soon receive the finest, largest, and best dressed doll that can be found anywhere."

I walked on again in the direction of Boston, and about 10 miles beyond I struck the Fitchburg railroad. It was now getting towards dawn and I say that I had better get under cover. Near the railroad track stood a barn and diagonally beyond a mill and a large house.

I decided to enter the barn and hide myself in the hayloft during the day. The door was unfastened. I climbed the ladder to the loft and concealed myself in the hay in such a manner that I could rise to my feet in case of need without making any preliminary movements.

I lay there for about half an hour. And then I heard somebody enter and begin to climb the ladder. I waited to hear some further movement, but there was no sound. I was on my feet with my revolver pointed, but as I peered down, there was nobody in sight.

I saw that the hayloft was no longer safe. I came to the barn door again, and as I did so I saw a man dodge around the corner of the barn. It was already daylight and beyond I could see four men coming from the house near the mill. I walked away to the railroad track, waved my hand to the men and dodged into the woods beyond.

I walked on through the woods in the direction of Fitchburg. I never felt greater energy before or since, and I piled up mile after mile. At about 2 o'clock in the afternoon I came upon a road just as a man with a buggy and a fast horse was passing. I hailed him and he gave me a lift for some 15 miles.

I walked on again, and at about 6 o'clock a light farm wagon came along, driven by a young Irishman. He took me as far as the outskirts of Fitchburg, where I got out and got to the other side of the city by way of side streets. From Fitchburg I made my way by hiring teams with some money which had been secretly slipped into my hand while I was being tried. At last I reached Boston and went at once to a friend's house, where I rested for a day and was then driven to Providence, where I took a train for New York.

I should say in connection with this first escape of mine from New Hampshire authorities that neither Wilder, the jailer, nor any member of his family had anything whatever to do with my break for freedom. Miss Wilder was a young woman of the greatest reserve toward me and knew little of me and nothing of my plans. I never made any attempt to win her to my side for the simple reason that I did not need either her help nor that of any member of her family. I knew well that with a revolver in my hands I had 99 chances out of 100 of intimidating the whole unarmed population of the town of Keene.

The most unfortunate personage in the whole affair was George M. White, a man entirely innocent of every part of the transaction. He had been drawn in by a series of peculiar circumstances over which he had no control and through the villainy of Cummings. From a man respected in the community in which he lived he was suddenly branded a crook, his property to the value of some $30,000 was attached and sold by the Walpole Bank people and when he at last escaped from the Keene jail he was a man without reputation or resources.

I have said in other reminiscences that White became a crook out of revenge and these were the circumstances that led him into the life of a criminal. No man ever had a greater provocation. It is not strange that in after years his particular delight was to rob banks in the state of New Hampshire. I estimate that the injustice done to White caused the community losses of at least $3,000,000 during his long career of a bank robber and burglar.

How I was rearrested and again broke jail and how I was brought to justice many years later I shall relate next Sunday. [Chapter 11]

11 HOW MARK SHINBORN AT LAST PAID THE PENALTY

I have related already the strange series of events which led to the robbery of the Walpole (N.H.) Bank and the peculiar incidents which made possible my escape from the Keene (N.H.) jail with half the population of the town at my heels.

The influence of the crime, however, did not cease to be felt simply because I was free, and it is the intent of this reminiscence to show how that relatively unimportant crime came to have a potent bearing upon my life through all the ups and downs of the 35 years which followed.

Not many months after my first escape I was rearrested in a manner as unusual as any that has come under my notice during my career. Again I was confined behind prison walls and again I made a break for liberty which was quite as sensational as that which had preceded it.

The details of my second escape have remained as much a mystery as any of my startling activities in the Granite state. There have been of course, many theories as to the way in which I outwitted the prison authorities, but until now the true story has never been told.

This account will clear up for the first time the circumstances of a case which had long been celebrated in police records and will set at rest many rumors which have borne heavily upon the reputations of officials who in realty had no hand at all in the affair.

It is a curious fact that the one man among my guards who had anything to do with my getaway was never suspected, while others who were entirely innocent remained under the stigma of public criticism for years.

Those who read this chronicle, I think, will have food for thought when they presume, as people will, that a mere accusation is proof of guilt. The worthlessness of mere circumstantial evidence was proven, I believe, in what I related of the connection of George M. White in my article last Sunday, and here again it is indicated in the fact that I lacked connivance from the prison officials who were generally supposed to have helped me.

I know of no other case like mine own in which a criminal was brought to final punishment for a crime after a lapse of three decades and a half. Between the actual break at Walpole and my last sentence to prison there was a lapse of years during which the methods of burglary had changed, and for that reason the case links me not only with the old days of "sneaking," key-safe manipulation and gunpowder blowing, but with the more modern era of nitroglycerine as well.

My experience as a result of the Walpole bank robbery might have discouraged any one less a professional burglar than I. To me, however, they were only the natural accidents of my way of life, and I was no sooner back in New York than I began to look about me for a new field of activity.

I made my headquarters at that time in a house in Bleeker street which was frequented by a number of crooks. I had never known these men before, but during the succeeding winter I joined them in an occasional job. Their work was for the most part devoted to blowing small safes, and the loot was never large.

When February 1866 arrived, I found myself out of funds, for the past months had been anything but profitable. Now, however, a minor crook, one "Steve" Brody, came to the gang with a story of what he called a "fine bank job" just over the Canadian border not far from St. Albans, Vt.

In view of our financial condition we were eager enough to get busy. As Brody described it, the whole affair promised to be the simplest thing in the world. The bank in question was situated in an ordinary dwelling and was without any particular protection. The safe was one of the oldest and flimsiest types and could be easily opened with no more intricate tool than a common jimmy. The only guardian was an aged retiree who did chores for the cashier and slept in the bank at night.

Although the project was not mine…with Brody I agreed to join "Red Bill" Wilson, "Jimmy" Ryan, and "Big Bill" McDavit, all hold-up men of some note. We went to St. Albans by train and there hired a large sleigh to take us to our destination.

It was a cold midwinter night and the snow lay on the ground in great drifts. All about the bank seemed quiet and at first view it looked as though all Brody's prophecies would come true. At the front there was a door leading from a porch into the bank room and here I stationed "Big Bill."

"Red Bill," Ryan and I then went around the house to a side door which gave upon a room that had once been the kitchen. From what Brody had told us, we knew that the handyman slept in a room, formerly a dining room, located just beyond. As I expected no difficulty in handling the decrepit watchman, I picked the lock without more ado and sneaked in alone, instructing Ryan to follow as soon as I squeaked like a mouse.

I walked softly through the kitchen into the room beyond and there found the old man lying on a lounge slumbering peacefully. I signaled to Ryan, who was so little cautious that he came blundering in as if he owned the house. Naturally the sound of his footfall aroused the sleeper, who started awake. I was at his side in a second and succeeded in frightening him so that he made no outcry. I spoke to the venerable guardian of the treasure kindly and told him he had nothing to fear as long as he made no noise. I then left him to the less tender mercies of Ryan.

As I crept out into the front hall I came upon a door which entered the bank room. While I was prowling about I caught the sound of subdued voices and retracing my steps, heard Ryan amusing himself by uttering bloodcurdling threats to his prisoner, who was absolutely harmless and needed no such treatment.

After I had quieted Ryan and reassured the victim of his peculiar humor, I went back to the front hall again and softly turned the knob of the bank room door. To my surprise, as I did so, I was answered by a man's voice calling out, "Who's there?"

"Let me in," I said gently.

"What do you want?" came the voice again.

"Open the door," I commanded in a louder tone, "or I'll shoot through it."

"Shoot and be damned to you," answered the voice as if it were a matter of fact request.

I saw at once that the jig was up and should have left the vicinity at all possible speed. The whole conversation, however, had been so unusual and unexpected and so tickled my sense of humor that I leaned against the jamb of the door and laughed. That man who seemed so careless of stray bullets was a man after my own heart.

While I stood there chuckling to myself, another man on the floor above shouted downstairs, "What in thunder is the matter down there?" The new voice recalled me to my senses and forgetting my little joke, I scurried of to Ryan and dragged him out of the house.

Just then there came the sound of scuffling on the front porch followed by a single shot. "Big Bill" was the target. He had seen the front door open and with his usual recklessness thrust his foot in to prevent it closing again. Then the man in the bank room fired and missed.

All this had only taken a few seconds and as Ryan and I stepped out into the open we spied "Red Bill" Wilson flattened against the side of the house just under one of the bank room windows. A window on the second floor flew up and then the window above Wilson's head opened.

Ryan and I were thigh-deep in drifts and to get to the road had to plow our way directly before those windows. As we floundered forward, the men at both windows opened fire at a range that could not have been more than eight or ten yards. The bullets whined by so close that I expected that either one of us would drop at any minute.

We had no time to shoot back, but Wilson who had recovered his presence of mind lifted his gun hand over his head and fired point blank into the lower window. This made a diversion long enough to permit Ryan and me to get by, and then we called to Wilson and McDavit. We set off at a run to the sleigh and reached it without being pursued.

There we found Brody, and as soon as McDavit spied him his temper broke out in good earnest. He grabbed the unfortunate "Steve," punched him with all the thoroughness possible, and then kicked him into a snowbank with a warning to get his facts a little more accurately when he tipped off a gang again. Leaving Brody to shift for himself, we drove off to St. Albans in anything but a pleasant frame of mind.

Ryan and I caught the first train for Rouse's Point and there changed cars for Malone. All the time Ryan had been complaining of a sharp pain in his shoulder, and when I examined him I found two holes in the sleeve of his coat where a bullet had gone out and in. Fortunately, however, he had received only a flesh wound, although he was bleeding freely. As I looked him over a little more closely I found that the skirt of his coat had been riddled with shot, and in one of his pockets was a .32-calibre bullet. For my own pat I had not been much damaged, although a piece of fur nicked out of my sealskin cap gave evidence of how near I had been to death.

It was then that there happened one of those incidents which not even the shrewdest crook can prevent. We were nearing Malone and I was congratulating myself on a clean getaway, when I looked up and saw four men grouped around me. Before I realized what was happening I was handcuffed.

It chanced that on the very same coach we had selected there was riding one of the men who had served on the jury when I was tried for the robbery of the Walpole Bank. It chanced, too, that in the smoking car were four deputy sheriffs who were just returning from the Clinton prison, near Plattsburgh, after taking a batch of convicts from Albany.

As soon as the former juror was convinced of my identity he slipped back to the smoker and notified the officers, who pounced on me before I could even put up a fight. I was taken at once to Albany and in due time the undersheriff of Cheshire county, N.H., arrived to take me back to Keene. I saw there was no use of making trouble, so I agreed to accompany him without the formality of extradition proceedings.

I think Sheriff Holt, my captor, believed that I had lost my mind, for whenever I thought of what had happened the night before, I laughed again. Holt looked at me in amazement and asked me what I found so funny about going back to prison for 10 years.

"I'm just thinking," I said, "of a pleasant invitation I had to shoot and be damned," and I grinned again.

In Keene, of course, I had become a sort of story book figure and naturally there was a large crowd to greet a former distinguished fellow resident when I arrived at the station. I was hustled through the mob to the jail, where I remained during the night. The following day I was taken to the pen at the Concord state prison.

I must say that I was treated with great kindness by the good warden Mayo at that time, and he even sent my dinner down from his own table to my cell. It was hard, nonetheless, to give up the joys of freedom at my age, and I began at once to plot a new escape.

I remember while I was at the prison I was honored by a visit from Gov. Smythe and a party of young women. I had quite a long conversation with the party. "Dear me," said one of the young women, "it does seem too bad that you should have to stay here 10 long years."

Even then I had a practical plan of escape in mind, and in a moment of bravado I answered, "Oh, that is nothing, for I do not intend to stay here."

"It's our duty to try to keep you," put in Gov. Smythe, and there the mater ended.

Just as the party turned to depart one of the girls lingered and whispered, "I do hope you will get out somehow."

"Never fear, madam," I whispered back.

The next day, however, I found an additional new lock on the door of my cell. I spoke of it jokingly to the warden and he replied somewhat apologetically by telling me the fable of the frog who was pelted with stones by boys.

"It may be fun for you boys," he quoted the frog, "but it's death to me."

I gathered he had no intention of playing the part of the frog if he could help it.

I was never more eager to be free. It may seem strange to those who have always been perfectly respectable that romance should enter the life of so desperate a character as Mark Shinborn, but there it was. During the winter I had fallen in love, not with a girl of the underworld, but with a young woman whose life was beyond reproach.

Everything that a woman could do to lead a man to a better life she had done for me, and yet, there I was behind prison walls, a branded criminal. I reproached myself that things had come to such a pass, but always ended by resolving that I would get away at any risk.

When at last I did escape, I returned to her again, and again she tried to make me a good man. But I was a crook, and nothing but a crook then. There could be but one outcome. I went my way at last and she went hers. Our paths were far apart.

All this, however, was an incentive such as I had never had before. On the day after my arrival I was assigned to the shop in which furniture was made by the prisoners and set to work at planing white wood panels. I was born with a mechanical turn and this was simple.

I recall one day when the contractor came to my bench and watched me at work. "Have you ever done this sort of work before?" he asked. "No, sir," I replied. "You lie," said he, turning on his heel.

A few months later the convict who had charge of jointing the bureaus and chests of drawers was discharged. I was promoted to his job and thus obtained a permanent location in the shop. That was what I desired, and I began at once to draw a small plan of the shop.

My workbench stood at a window which could be easily placed by counting the windows on either side of it from the ends of the building. The rear of the shop faced the back wall of the prison and between the shop wall and that surrounding the prison was a passage about 14 feet wide.

When all was ready, a friend of mine, "Billy" Maher, came to visit and when he shook hands with me I slipped the plan to him and instructed of how I hoped to effect my escape. The paper was folded so small that it passed from hand to hand unnoticed.

My first plan was in keeping with my desperation. My window was about halfway between the ends of the wall at the back of the shop. The greater part of the wall was unprotected, but a guard was stationed at each of the ends where it turned at right angles.

My idea was to have a rope ladder thrown over the 20-foot wall at the hour in the evening when the convicts stopped work. I decided that I would break from the line, clamber up the ladder and get over before the inside guards could marshal the other prisoners to their cells and come back for me.

There still remained the two guards on the wall who were armed with muskets. To take care of them I planned to have two of my friends on the outside whose duty it would be to keep up a close fire at the guards, not to hit but to confuse them.

It would be easy for my friends to know when to act because the time when the prisoners were to return to their cells was always announced by the ringing of a large bell in the prison yard, the clamor of which could be heard all over the neighborhood.

As soon as my waiting friends heard the bell, I planned that they should throw the ladder over the wall and at the same time begin shooting. The first shot would be a signal to me and I would drop my bucket, leave the line and make a dash for liberty.

This scheme had in it the elements of success, but had at the same time elements of great danger to me and to my liberators. My friends hesitated, and I set to work in another way. Through the influence of my friends and means which had been put at my disposal by them I won over one of the guards of my shop whom I shall call Blank for the sake of those relatives of his who may still be living.

He agreed to act as a go-between, carried a number of letters to my friends and brought me trustworthy information as to what they were doing in my behalf. After this correspondence had been going on for some time,

190

Blank came to me one day and said that he had a plan that looked like a good one. He told me that "Billy" Maher was again in Concord and asked what it would be worth if he helped me to get free.

I told him to arrange with Maher about the terms and wrote a brief note for him to take to Maher, telling the latter to find out just what the plan was before he passed over any money. Blank came back next day and told me that Maher had gone to New York to get some other crooks to help him.

Another few days passed and then another friend of mine called on me and slipped me a note which told me what was in the air and assured me that I could trust Blank. Six days later Blank got in touch with me and unfolded his plan, at the same time telling me that the money part of the transaction had been arranged.

Blank's idea was to bore a series of half-inch holes underneath the lower crossbar of the wooden gate of the prison yard. The holes would not be deep enough to be seen from the prison side, but still deep enough to make possible the forcing of the planks. The holes were to be placed close together and so arranged that they would be concealed by the overlapping crossbar which stood about two feet from the ground.

In this fashion the boards of the gate would be so weakened that by taking hold of them at the bottom I could break them off easily on a line with the holes. The boring was done according to schedule by one of my friends on the outside of the prison during the night before that on which I had determined to make my break for liberty.

Some days before that day of the final attempt arrived, Blank had secured a transfer to another shop in order that no suspicion should fall on him when the affair was discovered. He was replaced by a guard named Ordway who was by no means as keen as Blank and who absolutely nothing of the plan.

At last the important hour arrived. Blank had notified me to be ready. At 5 o'clock in the evening the bell clattered as usual, the long line of convicts formed in the shop and the customary lockstep march began toward the cells.

First of all we tramped once around the shop to pick up our buckets, and then the prisoners moved out toward the yard. Directly in front of me was a young fellow, who, like me, was doing a stretch of 10 years. He was always despondent and downcast and my heart was moved with pity for him.

At the risk of spoiling the whole plan, I whispered over his shoulder, "Say, if you will do just what I do, you will be a free man in a minute." With that I dropped my bucket, gave the man a tug at the arm and dashed for the gate in full view of everybody. The man hesitated and did not follow, but I made the 100 yards to the gate as fast as my legs would carry me.

All was in confusion for a minute. I seized the planks and to my joy they gave way at my first wrench. A second later a bullet whizzed past my head and kicked up the dust just in front of me.

Before another shot could be fired I dove through the little opening and was free. From the gate to the street was a little road about 40 yards in length. On one side of it stood the house occupied by the warden and his deputy and on the other a private house surrounded by a garden.

I looked around in vain for the carriage which my friends had promised to have ready, but none was in sight. With that I jumped the fence to the right into the garden, skirted the rear of the house, bending low. I passed within 30 yards of the dining room of the house. The window curtains were up, and as I glanced to one side I could see a large family eating supper. Strange to say no one of them looked up from their meal as I passed.

For a moment I crouched behind some shrubbery and then I spied an express wagon with a man and boy on the seat passing along the street in front of me. In a flash I saw what I must do. I resolved to run behind the wagon, climb to the seat, throw the driver off and then drive away myself.

I had just jumped the fence and was starting after the wagon when I saw a horse and buggy turn the corner from the direction of the prison. One look showed me that the driver was my friend, and without a second's hesitation I ran to meet the rig, clambered into the seat, and we were off at a breakneck clip towards Manchester.

I was no sooner seated than my friend passed me a navy revolver and then I felt as if the town belonged to me. Throughout the night we continued our flight as fast as the horse could go, and by daylight had reached a little roadside tavern where we fed the horse and got a meal for ourselves. There I changed my clothes, and hid my prison suit under a stone fence. I kept my cap, however, for a souvenir.

From there to Manchester was a long stretch and when we arrived the horse was exhausted. My friend sought out a livery stable where he left our rig and hired another. In the meantime I went to a barber shop for a shave and shampoo, and while I was being made more presentable the barber entertained me with the details of the escape of Mark Shinborn.

I did not dare to show up at any public place for breakfast, so that when my friend had had his own meal he brought me a large supply of sandwiches. We drove off again and in due time reached Boston, where I stopped at the house of the same man who had given me a place of refuge after my first escape. On the following day I was driven to Providence and from there took a train to New York.

It was a curious coincidence that the very night that I escaped from Concord, George M. White, who had been co-defendant with me at my trial for the Walpole Bank Robbery, had arranged to rob the bank at Keene.

Some months after my escape from the Keene jail, White had made a successful break for freedom. Although he had up to that time been a respectable hotel keeper, as soon as he was free he joined a band of crooks in New York and set to work to secure his revenge by a series of robberies in New Hampshire. If he had been successful with the Keene bank it would have been a double blow to the Cheshire county authorities.

As it turned out, however, White's gang were not able to carry out their plan and got back to New York from Keene the very day I arrived from Boston.

My escape from Concord in December, 1866, marked the beginning of my career as a successful bank burglar. Between that time and the year 1869 I robbed nine out of eleven banks which I attempted, and secured a share in loot ranging from $50,000 to $1,900,000.

In 1870 I was a man of wealth, with a fortune close to $500,000. In that year I married and went over to Europe, where I had purchased an estate, and settled down for a number of years to the life of a landed proprietor. My career there would make an interesting story in itself, but has no place in this reminiscence.

Suffice it to say that by 1892 my fortune had been lost, and in order to get a living I was forced to return to my old life as a crook. I came back to New York a man past middle age. In the years that had gone by conditions in this country had changed. Most of the banks were closely guarded and the country institutions no longer carried large sums of money. Besides, my age and physical condition made it impossible for me to do the "sneak" work for which I was once famous.

At first I turned my attention to the perfecting of an invention, hoping that the success of this would make it possible for me to give up the life of a crook, but after two years I was forced to abandon my work for lack of funds.

Seeing that there was nothing I could do but follow my old trade of a burglar, I began to study the newer methods. The use of dynamite for safe-blowing had come into vogue and with my knowledge of safes and locks I improved on some of the systems used by the latter-day burglars.

Although I was no longer active as of yore, I took in a partner and we started on the warpath, turning our attention to post offices and small banks. My first job, a country bank, netted me $3000, my second brought me $15,000, my third proved a failure, and my fourth led to my arrest and brought to life again the old robbery of the Walpole Bank, then more than a generation old.

The job which led to this last arrest was an attempted break at the National Bank of Middleburgh, in Schoharie county, N.Y. The building was a solid affair of one story with a store on one side and a vacant lot on the other. Directly opposite was a dwelling, on the second floor of which lived a widow and her daughter.

This latter house led to my failure, for it was possible to look down from the upper rooms into the bank and see the vault, in front of which a light was kept burning all night. I found it easy to enter the building through a side window while my partner remained outside on guard.

I had come well prepared for my work with a fine set of tools of the best make packed away in a swell little leather handbag. My drills were of the finest, my brace was extra small and was so arranged that it could be disjointed and carried in the pocket, while my sectional jimmy was only 20 inches long when jointed.

It was the first job in which I had ever used nitroglycerine. This I carried in a small flask, while some cotton, detonating caps and fuse completed my outfit. It was a simple process. I drilled a hole three-eighths of an inch in diameter about a half-inch above the spindle of the combination lock, shoved in some cotton moistened with the explosive, then squirted in a little more of the nitroglycerine and fitted the cap and fuse.

I touched off the fuse and then stepped around the corner of the vault. Compared with the old-fashioned gunpowder explosions of my earlier years this one was as the report of a revolver to the boom of a cannon. The lock was blown off cleanly and all I had to do to open the door was turn the bolt handle.

The second vault door was served in the same way, but the burglar-proof safe inside was a more difficult problem, although there was no drilling to do. I knocked off the combination and poured the nitroglycerine in through the spindle in the lock. The explosive, however, did not reach the lock, but spread down between the steel plates of the door which was three inches through. The explosion which followed split the door in halves and threw the outer half on the floor. I knew that one more charge would do the trick and was about to proceed when I was warned of trouble by my partner.

The woman in the house across the street had been awakened by the repeated reports. She went to her window and looked directly down upon me where I was working. At last she came downstairs, opened the street door and peered out. It was then that my partner signaled to me. I left my work at once and came out. When my partner told me what he had seen I sneaked across the street and heard footsteps going upstairs inside.

I saw at once that it would not be long before the alarm was given and as it was almost dawn I decided to abandon the job and get away as soon as possible. My partner and I hastened to the railroad where we stole a handcar and worked our way to a patch of woods some six miles further on. There we remained all day and then went 10 miles further on.

By this time my partner was tired out and left me to go to a hotel in a little town nearby. He took my tools with him and when he was arrested on suspicion on the following morning the tools were damaging evidence against him.

I managed to make my way back to New York, but the safety I was sure of in the sixties was no longer a fact. Some six weeks later as I was walking along Seventh avenue I was surrounded by five detectives and placed under arrest. The warrant bore the name Mark Shinborn, but I insisted it was a case of mistaken identity.

My partner pleaded guilty, but I went to trial and was convicted. My case was then appealed, and the supreme court granted me a new trial. My defense throughout was that I had not been Shinborn, although the newspapers made much of my arrest on that supposition and gave detailed accounts of my character as the "King of Burglars."

On the day before my second trial my lawyer had a talk with the county authorities, who were not anxious for the expense and bother of another hearing. The state's attorney suggested that I should make a plea of guilty on the charge of attempting to break jail, for which a fine of $250 would be imposed, and then said that the burglary case would be dropped.

I was convinced, however, that the evidence against me was very flimsy and I thought that I would be surely acquitted on my second trial. Accordingly, when my lawyer came to me with his new proposition, I rejected it and chose rather to go to trial again.

In that I made the greatest mistake of my life, for when I was brought to the bar I was convicted promptly, or rather "railroaded," as the underworld phrase has it when a man is sent away on insufficient evidence. I was confined in the state prison at Dannemora, where I must admit I was well treated.

My term expired Oct. 10, 1900, but my troubles were by no means over. The ancient bogey of the Walpole robbery arose once more to plague me, and I was no sooner discharged than the sheriff of Cheshire county, N.H. appeared on the scene with a requisition warrant.

I was taken to the Plattsburgh jail and there my counsel instituted habeas corpus proceedings, but without avail. On Nov. 11 of the same year I was given into the custody of Sheriff Tuttle of Keene and Warden Cox of Concord.

In the proceedings which followed the same New York detective whose evidence had convicted me at my trial years before was once again my Nemesis. He it was whom I have accused as the man who passed me the revolver in the Keene jail. He is now dead and there is no occasion for making his name public.

His action at my trial in the sixties had made him persona non grata, although that isn't what we called it among crooks, with certain other officials in the New York police headquarters. After that he was never assigned to any important duty, although he was known familiarly among the city pickpockets.

Not long afterwards certain of the detectives who were on closer terms with the underworld put up a job on him so that he was given his "rake-off" in marked money. He was arrested and the marked bills found. The case, however, was hushed up and he was allowed to resign from the force.

Later he became a private detective for a New York hotel and occupied that position during the years of my prosperity in New York. I had occasional dealings with him, but after 1867 never saw him again until the year 1900 when his memory of me made possible my identification as Mark Shinborn, although I declared stoutly that I was not the celebrated crook he said I was.

The authorities, however, were satisfied that I was the robber of the Walpole Bank, and despite all my efforts I was sentenced to pay the penalty for my first crime in New Hampshire. I was not at liberty again until 1908.

During my imprisonment at Concord I made several attempts to have my case reopened, but without success. When I was brought back to New Hampshire after my surrender by New York officials I was placed in a hack and hurried at once to the penitentiary.

My defense from the time of my arrest for the Middleburgh bank attempt had been that I was not Mark Shinborn, that my real names was that which I use at present, and that I was the victim of mistaken identity. I believed that in view of this claim I should have been given a hearing before a magistrate in New Hampshire.

There were other technicalities upon which I relied. In 1866, when I made my escape from the prison at Concord, it was a rule of law in New York state that in the event of an escape of a prisoner in that state his time of sentence continued just as if he had remained a prisoner. In other words, a convict could not be returned to prison if he remained free a number of years equal to the term of his original sentence.

I had maintained that, inasmuch as I had been at liberty for 34 years, I could not be held liable for my old crime, at least so far as New York was concerned, and that I could not, therefore, be extradited from that state and turned over to New Hampshire, no matter what might be the law of the latter commonwealth.

I had understood, too, that the first requisition made for me was not on the ground of robbery, but for the offence of breaking prison. In 1866, however, there was no law in New Hampshire which covered that offence. It was not until later that such a law was enacted. My claim on that head was that the law which had been passed after my escape could not touch me, for the reason that it would thus become retroactive and would infringe upon my rights under the United States constitution. I have been given to understand that an attempt was made to have me indicted for breaking jail, but that the proposition was held not to be legal.

I fought the case in Plattsburgh in 1900 on habeas corpus proceedings as far as my means would allow, but failed to make out my defense. I was turned over to the New Hampshire authorities, and the $1000 reward, which had been offered for me in 1866 and still remained in force, was paid to a former detective who had been interested in my earlier arrest.

I arrived at the Concord prison Nov. 11, 1900. As usual, my "pedigree" was first taken, and then I was ordered to undress in the office and was taken to a bathtub nearby. I was directed to get into the tub "quick" and to "hurry up." I stepped in and found that there was about two inches of water in the bottom.

I had no sooner seated myself, however, and had begun to sprinkle myself with water than I was directed to "jump out" again. Realizing that my guardians meant business from their attitude toward me, I did not delay in obeying. As I stepped to the floor I reached for a towel which hung close at hand, but before I could grasp it one of my captors broke in and to me to "put these clothes on quick."

I was given my prison garb, a shirt, trousers, socks, shoes, jacket and cap. One of the men then grabbed me by the shirt close to the throat, and while the other stood by demanded roughly: "Now will you behave yourself while you're in this prison?" I was surprised and for the moment was speechless. The first man then gave me another shake. "Answer quick," he commanded. "Will you behave yourself?" I recovered myself enough to answer: "Certainly I will."

Meanwhile my body remained wet from my dip in the bathtub and gave me a very uncomfortable sensation when I was taken to the cold cell to which I had been assigned on the ground floor of the prison.

When morning came I was marched to the shop where chairs were made, and while standing there facing a wall I felt a shock of sickness come over me not unlike an apoplectic attack. This I traced to my condition when I was placed in my cell on the previous night.

I was put to work, however, and was told that I must not let my eyes wander. I was so placed that I had a large part of the shop before my eyes, but I do not remember that I was at all eager to look about me. My guard seemed to think that I was curious, for he delighted, apparently, in nagging me for not keeping my eyes downcast. How I could do otherwise than I did I do not know, for my labor was so arranged that my hands were employed on a level with my eyes.

One of the peculiar ordeals of the prison came on the weekly bath day. Then gangs of six were marched through the yard, even in the coldest weather. Each man was obliged to remove his socks and carry them in his hands.

Once at the bath-house the prisoner was ordered to disrobe in quick time and to get at once into the tub. As a rule the water was about two inches deep and was always warm. When the man had seated himself another convict gave him a swirl down the back with a wet cloth, and at the end of about 20 seconds the guard called: "Out!" A few hasty passes over the body with a towel completed the performance, and then the prisoners hastened to dress again and were back at the shop at the same quickstep in which they had come.

Lest it may be said that I am exaggerating I will state that I have frequently counted the seconds during my bath, and the largest number I ever tallied was 28.

I have spent many years in prison, and I believe I am well qualified to speak of conditions, because I have a fair basis for comparison. There were a number of things which were unusual besides our method of bathing. One thing that touched me nearly was the type of shoe which the convicts were compelled to wear. These were made of very stiff, inflexible leather and were crudely finished, so that they were often rough and lumpy on the inside. I know that I suffered intensely from the pain they caused in my feet.

Even for prison fare the food was bad as a rule. At times the bread was soggy, at other times touched with blue mold, and for the most part only passable. Fresh meat was never served except on one or two of the yearly holidays. In amount the meals were usually insufficient, at least I found them so, and a goodly portion of them were made up of bread and molasses. Under Warden Cox we were allowed a pint of milk daily, but this was discontinued under Warden Scott.

I think, however, that the most pitiable situation with which I came in contact was the method of handling sick prisoners. With this phase I have good reason to be familiar. I have already mentioned my first attack of dizziness. This was followed during two years by a sort of neuralgia from which I suffered, especially during the night.

After a period of practical sleeplessness I asked to be allowed to see the doctor. The physician was in the cell hall every day of the week except Sundays. His patients were brought in one by one from the shop and lined up with their faces against the wall. As a man's turn arrived the deputy touched him with a cane and then the patient faced about.

It was difficult for a man who stood under the eyes of his guard to explain his case satisfactorily. From time to time the official made a slighting remark, generally to the effect that the patient was shamming and had nothing the matter with him. Judging from my own case, this was always a trying time, and I am convinced that not a few of the men became confused and were not able to give anything like a correct description of their symptoms.

When a prisoner was under the doctor's care every word on the part of the prison authorities made him feel that he was considered a fraud. Few of us ever reached the hospital, and those who did seldom returned. They were taken there to die.

Prison officials told me that the sick were better in the cells than in the hospital. Even in the winter the windows of the hall were opened wide every day as soon as the men had gone to the shop, and the sick prisoner in his cell was left without protection from the cold air.

Here is a case: A convict in cell No. 9 fell sick and was allowed to see the doctor two or three times. Each time, however, he was sent back to the shop. A little later he fainted in the line and was removed to his cell. The next day, however, he was sent again to the shop. He still claimed to be sick, and on the following day was punished for his behavior by being hung up in handcuffs with his feet off the floor.

When he returned to the shop he fainted once more and was taken to his cell. On the following day he became delirious and was carried to the hospital. That was the last I ever saw of him. I have often though that the man who invented the state prison system in New Hampshire was a genius in refined cruelty, and I have sometimes wondered that men could be found to carry it out. During my stay there was no provision made for exercising in the prison yard, a practice which is general in other prisons, both in this country and in Europe.

As soon as I became an inmate I began my attempt to secure legal assistance. Once every two months I was allowed to write a letter, but it was nearly two years before I succeeded in getting a lawyer to come to see me. When at last an attorney came to visit me the warden was on hand, and said as least as much as anybody during the conference.

I wished to be taken before a judge on a writ of habeas corpus to raise the question whether I had been properly imprisoned without being given a hearing in New Hampshire. Of course I denied still that I was Shinborn, but that was not my main contention.

I agreed to pay the lawyer $40, all the money that the warden held for me. He informed me later that the only ground upon which I could be brought to court was on a question of identity. I refused to make a contest on that ground, and refused to pay my $40 to the lawyer.

I appealed directly to the United States district court, and a lawyer was recommended, but I found that the court held the same view as to the scope of my case. Later I appealed to the United States circuit court, but it was again decided that the only issue was one of identity.

I had been in prison seven years when I had got to that point. I then thought of trying the United States supreme court, but before I accomplished anything in that direction I was reported by the shop guard for a minor infraction of the rules, and as punishment I was not allowed to write anything further during the rest of my term in the prison.

ABOUT THIS TEXT

Schoenbein's articles as printed in the *Boston Herald* contained inconsistent spellings and compound word forms, some representing archaic or British usage. Those have been changed in this text to avoid distraction to contemporary readers. Similarly, several place names he mentions as ending in "-burg" have since adopted the spelling "-burgh," and those, too have been changed to accommodate current usage. His use of short paragraph structure suited newspaper publication. That convention has been preserved.

www.ingramcontent.com/pod-product-compliance
Lightning Source LLC
La Vergne TN
LVHW051627080426
835511LV00016B/2218